In Praise of Gratitude

IN PRAISE OF

Books by Robert Raynolds

BY

COMPANION BOOKS

The Choice to Love

In Praise of Gratitude

NOVELS

Brothers in the West

Saunders Oak

Fortune

May Bretton

The Obscure Enemy

Paquita

The Sinner of Saint Ambrose

The Quality of Quiros

Far Flight of Love

Publishers

DRAMA

Boadicea (verse)

GRATITUDE

An Invitation to Trust in Life

ROBERT RAYNOLDS

Harper & Brothers   *New York*

Contents

7

Book Six 🖈 *Gratitude and Suffering*

Book Seven 🖈 *The Beatitude of a Lived Life*

Book Eight 🖈 *Song of Heart*

❧❧ INVITATION

For a Man—for a Woman—for a Child

When I was a child I saw something more than once that each time made my heart sing with sudden laughter. It was a warm and tender glow lighting up my mother's face, it was a swift and shining light of open trust and happy strength that moved her body as in music and in dance; and her voice would sing to the child I was, telling me not why or wherefore, but telling me the greatest thing:

"Oh, Bobby! I am so grateful!"

And I knew that gratitude was laughter in her heart, pouring out and filling my heart with laughter, too.

When I was a young man one of the loveliest things that ever happened to me was this: I had returned to New York after a year in Mexico. I had the address of a young woman I had met on my way to Mexico months before, and memories of loveliness about her. I went to a building strange to me and rang the bell at a door I had never seen before. And she opened the door, and suddenly as she saw me a change of light came over her face and her body rose out of the routine of answering a doorbell into free upspring of dancing life, and she said:

"I am glad to see you!"

She said it in every light and motion and sound of her whole being.

And I knew that gratitude had suddenly flooded her heart with blessing, and her gratitude had overflowed and blessed my heart.

And I knew that gratitude is a blessing that we give to one another.

When she and I had grandchildren, one of the tenderest things that ever touched me was the body and life of a grandchild coming to sit in my lap and listen with me to music. I was sitting in a big chair in my studio, with a Mozart record playing, and he came in the door with the watchful approach of an alert and sensitive being, poised for peril, poised for welcome. Perhaps I smiled a smile that said:

"Bobby, I'm glad you're here!"

His dusky eyes stopped watching for signs of peril or signs of welcome and lit up with mischief and delight; and he came across the room to music and climbed into my lap; and he laid his cheek against my breast and touched my face tenderly with fingers bestowing the pure communion of a child's caress; and I put my arm around him. Neither of us said a word, and we sat there in quiet joy and listened to music.

I was grateful that he had come; he was grateful that I had welcomed him.

And I knew that gratitude was tenderness of responsible communion between us.

One of the most healing things that ever healed my heart of painful wound came upon a day in Springtime, now in the depth of later years when it is too late not to have failed. In strain of suffering and burn of despair I went into a woodland by a waterfall to lay my body and my sorrow on the ground. And I lay down like an uncreated, lean, and sluggish thing, and all alone, that was not a man. And there in the music of woodland and water and in the dancing dapple of springtide light, all of a sudden and yet with that slow suddenness of divine approach, my whole being was flooded with a knowing that I was immeasurably not alone, but created and now created anew in the midst of being, created in the presence of God and by the touch of God and by the gratitude of God. And I rose from sorrow on the ground in the rise and motion and delight of gratitude.

And I knew that gratitude is our home in the presence of God, and that gratitude is God's declaration of life.

These are only a beginning of hundreds of little stories from my life, and they tell me this: That no man can be grateful to himself, but sings and lives his gratitude to others and to God. They tell me that gratitude is laughter in our heart, is blessing flowing out of our heart, is tenderness entrusting us to one another, is our living harmony with the music of God.

And so I am moved to sing my praise of gratitude to others and to God. And here I say and sing it, for a man, for a woman, for a child, in the only way I know, by the telling of my gratitude in song and story, in sayings from my heart and meditations from my life, by parable and vision and thought and essay and prayer. It goes by name of a book, but what it really is is a man's living act of gratitude offered out of his life to others and to God.

And so, to read it is more than just reading; it is to join communion with another in gratitude for living.

I invite a man and a woman and a child to become my companion in gratitude, in the spirit of laughter, of blessing, of tenderness, and of rising from sorrow into renewal of life in the presence of God—in the spirit of the little stories I have just told.

For this is the spirit in which all the book is told.

Book One

Child of the Heart

1 ❧❧ Do You Know the Wind?

A Vision

*Do you know the wind blowing at night among all the stars?
Who can rise in the morning and step out on the earth in the mist
before dawn, and say it is himself that established the earth and
brings on the day? Do you rise in the morning and step out on
the earth in the mist before dawn, and rejoice in the Other, Who
brings on the day? Who shall ever disclose his full gratitude for
the abundance of God in the night and the day? Our earth is one
of the stars among all the stars of heaven, and, in truth, there is
no other place but heaven, and no other time but eternity. How
shall the heart of a man be great enough to rejoice in his gratitude
for the abundance of God? How shall the voice of a man be tender
enough to sing his consonance with God?*

2 ❧❧ Morning Child

A Memory

Have you seen a naked child, slowly, softly and wobbling adrowse
in the cool shadow of the doorway, rubbing stillness and sleep
from the dreamy pools of his eyes with push and turn of his tender
fists? And then his plump arms hang still and his head turns and
his eyes awaken with attentive wonder to morning in the sky and
dew of morning sparkling on the grass. Then spontaneous gratitude
alerts the living mystery of his body and life out of sleepy laxness
into dance, and gratitude comes smiling up from his heart to his
lips and wakes a wild intent suddenly aglow in his eyes. How

17

lovely with startled life he now becomes, while gratitude attunes his delighted heart and wholeness to the moving finger of God in new creation in the shine of morning before his face! So that he bursts, born anew into the day, out of the shadow of all slumber into the splendor of entire light. And he runs and tumbles and chortles his wild, wild glee across the spongy turf, with splash of dew and green blades of grass adorning the bright flash of his naked feet, and he wheels a turn among the dancing flowers, he and they drenched in shining shower of morning sun and fragrant air; and he whoops his merry mirth, not afraid of bumblebees!

Suddenly, in creative poise of man's mysterious intelligence, man's strange gift, so like a power, of naming, touching, and affirming with delight all that he meets, he touches a flower with the shining finger tip of his released and communing love, and all the world lives in that holy moment and touch, drawn together in radiant blessing, wherein the touch of God, through the intelligent finger of a grateful child, has moved once more in new creation.

3 ❧ Praise of Gratitude

Sayings of the Heart

Gratitude is illumination.
Gratitude is the form of a smiling mind.
Gratitude is the pulse of a singing heart.
Gratitude is the root of love.
Gratitude is singing balance in all the body.
Gratitude is the dawn of joy.
Gratitude is the great and ready peace of being a man.
Gratitude is our welcome to all the world.
Gratitude reveals great meanings in our day, in our doing, in our sudden joy.
Gratitude is the sacred awakening of our consonance with God.
Gratitude is our rejoicing and our song of heart.

Gratitude is our great affirmation of life.
Gratitude is a region of spirit in which we may dwell.
Gratitude is our home in the presence of God.

4 ❧ *Region of Spirit*

An Essay

Gratitude is a region of spirit.

It is a region of spirit in which no one is unwelcome and no one lives alone.

Gratitude is more than a word to be looked up in a dictionary. It is neither explained nor explained away by a few words of definition, such as "an expression of thanks for benefits received." One psychologist calls it "one of the sentiments," but that is not enough. Another calls it "a binary emotion composed of tenderness and negative self-feeling"; tender it is, robust it surely is, but negative self-feeling it surely is not, for it is feeling of relation aboundingly released; and to pigeonhole it as an emotion composed of two other emotions is like pretending to pigeonhole the grandeur and flow of the Mississippi River by saying it is composed of the confluence of the Missouri and the Tennessee, or like defining marriage in its living mystery as a binary social unit composed of a man and a woman. Gratitude is a profound condition of life lived in a generous, sane, and creative region of spirit. Gratitude is a shining great river of human life, on which the spirit and work and fulfillment of man is borne from mystic mountains of origin into the entire enfolding sea of consonance with God.

Gratitude is a region of spirit wherein a man may dwell. It is here, and not remote in space. It is now, and not backwards or forwards in time. And it is communion, not solitude.

One of the most compelling questions you may ask about a man any day of his life is this: "Where is he now?" And of yourself, "Where am I now?" It is God's question, asked of man: "Adam, where art thou?" This does not mean his physical address, city, town, or country, or whether he is high in a plane or snug in a ship or underground in a mine, not among the lotus with Ulysses nor with Adam among the asphodels of Paradise. It is a question of a man's spiritual address. Where is he now? In what region of spirit? Good or foul? Sane or fearful? In sweet converse among aspiring souls or in leering disport among the horrid sisters of Beelzebub? Orestes flying from the Furies across wasteland's bitter ground, or Francis reclined in grateful gathering peace, beneath an olive tree?

To make it modern, suppose you are a passenger in a transport plane in high flight and foul weather, and the great tides of stormy air sway and lift and drop the plane, and lightning gives a ghastly light to tumbling shapes of cloud, and you ask yourself: "Where is the pilot now?" Physically, you know, he is in the cockpit; you can see his shoulders and head and the radio earphones clamped to his ears, while he listens and tells, listens and tells, in incredible communication with voices far away. But you want to know in what region of spirit the man is alive? Is he flying ten minutes behind his plane in moody anger at some event a thousand miles behind this present storm, back there on the ground in the morning? Is he flying ahead of his plane, irresponsible of this wild vortex of here and now, in a tizzy of expectation of kissing a girl a thousand miles ahead on earth in the evening? Is he in a region of spirit of distraction of any sort? Or is he in the region of spirit of man's gratitude for man's intelligence, skill, and courage, in serene control of his responsible job? Where he is in region of spirit is now influencing every life in the plane, including his own. Is he in the region of life or the region of death? Well would it be if he is a whole man hallowing his work here and now, alert to the storm, skilled in the powers of the craft he pilots, responsible to each life concerned, with gratitude for tense, high, and immediate reality rousing up his heart to steady, fearless, and responsible joy! And thou, oh passenger? Are you chattering fear against the back of the pilot's head and into every face you see, building within the plane as perilous a storm as already rages without? Are you scolding the day, the company, the plane, the pilot, the hour, down along the path of ruin? Or have you gratitude enough for the wonder of life at all to add to the strength of life needed now?

We have plenty of moods and fancies in the livelong day of our lives that move us up and down and round about in our doing with things and our dealings with one another. We have our blue Mondays and our days of laughter, our curiosity about this, our ambition for that, some courage here or some anxiety there, now boredom, now delight, a mood of warm memory or a mood of high expectation. We go at our work with intent and effective skill, play our game in alert competition, stick to our point with intelligence and integrity, sometimes envy, sometimes admire, sometimes laze in the sun, hate with a vengeance, or love with a difference.

But there are two great regions of spirit we may enter, either of which may grasp, mold, and encompass our living of our life in this world: the region of gratitude or the region of resentment. It makes a profound difference in the measure and meaning of a lived human life in which of these regions we dwell. If we live in this world at all, we live in one of these regions or the other—and, of course, sometimes in one and sometimes in the other. There may be some souls who live not in this world but in regions other than daily mortal, regions of Nirvana or of detached intellect or regions of some great hereafter or, with reality lost, are enthralled in dreaming; but most of us live most of our lives in this world, either in gratitude or in resentment. And if we live in gratitude, then the cosmos is our habitable home, and we cherish living and help the living of others. If we live in resentment, we fight out a valueless existence in a hostile universe, sharp as Goneril and Regan hounding their old father Lear to his insane death, and consign ourselves to a withered heart.

Whom do we know toward whom to turn our hearts that we do not doubt lived in gratitude of being and in grateful consonance with God? Why, Socrates in his sanity, Buddha in his compassion,

Christ in his love. I have traveled here and there about our earth, and I never stayed in any town so small that there was not in it a man and a woman and a child living in the region of spirit of gratitude: I have been a passing stranger, and their smiles have lifted me up.

And no man is alone in the region of gratitude. For sanity, compassion, and love are what gratitude gives to our life together.

5 ❧ Our Age of Resentment

A Lament

There has been a flight of intelligence into the realms of destruction. Now is an age of resentment.

Great voices of gratitude are few in our age. The noblest one I know is that of Martin Buber, who profoundly believes in hallowing the day of our life and the work of our life and the meetings of our life as fully as we can to the measure of our life, which is a vision founded in gratitude for our consonance with God.

But the voices of resentment are legion. Woman resents her position; man resents his job. Science resents religion; religion resents science. There has been a centuries-long flight of high human intelligence into the region of resentment and the camps of attack. This is the day of the Great Against. We are told a lot about cultural and moral relativity, as if there were no values, no guilt, no sin, but the tellers of the tale cancel out what they say about there being no values, no guilt, no sin by the furious passion with which they attack the values of others, the guilt of others, the sin of others. It is a grievous thing when high intelligence turns to scorn and scolding as its major concern. The minister and Calvin Coolidge were both against sin; great countries are roaring against the sins of one another; the skeptical attack the sin of faith; the sophisticated attack the sin of decency; the pragmatic attack the sin of value; the despairing attack the sin of meaning; politics and ideology attack the sin of their opponents. It is a grievous thing when high human intelligence flees into fury of scorn and scolding, seeks subtle methods of propagandizing anger, calls for the banding together of victims, and toils for another and another breakthrough into vaster idiocy in fabricating weapons of slaughter. We are gone a little mad following this flight of proud human intelligence into turmoil, strife, and deepening trouble under the banner of the Great Against.

Is is not a grievous use of our intelligence to flay the sins of others and proclaim the villainy of God?

Gratitude gives us into sweet courtesy of living with earth and people and God. But resentment is a destructive scold, rendering ourselves and others faceless, and blinding fertile beauty out of all the world.

Scolding digs a deep pit. However hot the words, scolding is sharp cold work. The pit it digs never did anyone any good. This is surely the pit of Sisyphus, and misery is the stone heavy in our heart that we try and fail to roll up out of it. The immediate scolding of another person looking at us digs good ground from under us, and our own scolding of another makes a deeper hole. But here, between I and Thou, is grateful daily kindness possible, too, to fill in the ground intemperately gouged away, and to establish trust and home again between us,—between the whole presence of the I and the whole presence of the Thou, in direct reality of relation.

But what of the temper of the times we live in? Bitter embrace of wrongs and angers seems to have scolded gratitude out of countenance. Two large dictionaries of modern psychology I have looked in do not either one of them even contain the word "gratitude," though many a neurosis, anger, fear, and destructive phase of psyche is named, offered and defined. The library in one of our largest universities contains in its card catalogue, listing tens of thousands of books in that library, not one card for a book with "gratitude" its title. A minister tells me that the dictionary of theology he uses in his work has no listing for the word "gratitude." Can you have psychic health without gratitude? Can you have wisdom without gratitude? Can you have religion without gratitude?

Gratitude and love nourish our human life. Each season brings new flowering of many books on love; but the years pass and the centuries wear away, and no man seems to rise among us to sing his praise of gratitude. Can you have love without gratitude? Gratitude is a first blessing. Gratitude is my home in the presence of God. When I am not grateful, I have no home and cannot love.

What has happened to gratitude? It is as if man had stopped making and stopped sharing a loaf of hallowed bread. What, in fact, has happened to contemporary man that turns him away from gratitude? Do we think life is so dreadful that we are not grateful for it? De we believe the grisly chatter that calls life a meaningless accident? Do we think we are so wondrous in ourselves that we can delight in no thanks to any other? That there is no other, but only objects shaped like men and trees and stars and lobsters for us to classify and use and poke at? That there is no Other, but only meaningless nothing instead of God? Are we so busy doing and doing and doing (like the Witches in Macbeth) that we dare not pause for gratitude lest our passionate brew lose its bubble and froth?

What a nasty scold is the noise of the world we now are making! It is the noise of man, angry, alienated, and faceless in resentment. The dominions and powers of this world are scolding one another; the politicians, the writers, the teachers, the preachers, the commentators are scolding, scolding. The leaders are scolding and the followers are scolding. Teachers and priests are scolding; pupils and parishioners are scolding. Doctors are scolding and patients are scolding. Parents are scolding and children are scolding. Sour grapes is the wine of the gnashing of our teeth. In a frenzy of demanding something more, something different, something better, something easier, something our way not your way, something ours not yours, something of yours to be ours, the spirit of man today is gouging and bulldozing us all into a pit of wrath and hell, with a stigma of guilt and enmity put upon the face of anyone who does not become faceless and scold harder, dig deeper. In resentment we scold and are scolded out of countenance, and so become faceless, homeless, loveless, profoundly alienated one from another, but all wrapped together in the dark package of anger, sealed with the seal of the Great Against. We live in an ice-age and deep-freeze of cold scolding.

We are in desperate need of firm ground of gratitude to give us standing together in light again, with peace and joy of life returned to our hearts again, and giving us back our human faces and our human warmth.

But the sayings against gratitude are hard sayings; we hear them any day, and we shudder and turn away from gratitude. In saying here and there that I was now engaged in a work in praise of gratitude, I have been told by some that I was praising an ultimate sin, that gratitude is a greater sin against man set free than even faith or decency or value or meaning. It is indeed the sin of praising God; and to man set free—by his own thought set free— any praise except unto himself is sin. All else he abhors.

The hard sayings against gratitude are three:

That gratitude is something which we, as being superior, have a right to expect and demand from man and dog.

That gratitude is a humiliating demand made upon us, rendering us inferior and servile, by one of greater power, man or God.

That gratitude is a cynical tool we may use to wrest something we want out of the grasp of another.

Now these three hard sayings are profoundly true of fear of companionship; and not one of them is true of gratitude. We are terrified of being less than somebody else. We are terrified of not being superior to someone else. Man is terrified of not being greater than God. And we fear that gratitude may open the gates of these terrors and flood down ruin upon our lonely and separate pride. But gratitude turns our life in trust and companionship toward man and woman and child, toward earth and creature and God.

Gratitude in our own heart opens us to communion in responsible tenderness. Our own gratitude makes us immeasurably not alone, and establishes our life and our death in harmony with reality.

And now, in our age of resentment, who shall first put foot into the region of gratitude?

Not another, to welcome me; but myself, to welcome him.

I shall step into the region of the spirit of gratitude, and welcome thee.

I do so.

The child of my heart steps into the joy of the morning and welcomes thee.

6 ❧ *Child of the Heart*

An Essay

There is a sense of absolute joy in the gratitude of innocence. There is a child in the heart of each of us who knows no evil and has no need of prayer.

But the heart of a man is a family of persons: the man of dreams, the man of work, the man of play, the man of thought, the man of aspiration, the man as son, as lover, as father, the confident man and the tragic man, man practical and man poet, *homo lupus* and *homo sanctus,* the man of the world and the man of God—and the little child of the heart shall lead them. There is a family just the same in the heart of a woman, in many persons like those in the family of a man's heart, but some quite other, such as woman beloved, woman mother, *dolorosa, pietà, genetrix, sancta.* And as in the family of the heart of a man, so in this family of the heart of a woman, the innocent child shall lead them. And all these persons, except only the child of the heart, may know evil, and they shall have need of prayer. But gratitude is established in absolute joy in the child of our heart.

The child of our heart is the child in us who is never absent from God. Whether he moves into the deep and wonder of the night or steps into the joy of the morning, he responds with his life in a deep, rich, and strenuous involvement with the poetry of the world. He ventures into the mystery of reality and dwells in the ineffable presence of God.

This child of our heart is something of a nuisance to our practical living. The advancement, comfort, and security of self are not his aim. Perilous delight of entire living is the creative gratitude that frees and moves him. Instead of selling a bill of goods, he turns to another to become a friend; he is responsible to reality and will live a reality instead of earning a living; the child in the heart of a woman will pass up a committee to go mother a child, and instead of adorning her hair and packaging her body in silk will turn away from every mirror directly to set joy in the heart of a man. The other persons in the family of the heart have much ado in their daily doings to escape, fence off, avoid the perilous, creative, and grateful wonder that moves this child of our heart to divine adventure.

Sometimes a monkey wrench gets dropped into the works; sometimes a cake gets burned in the oven.

But this child is the most divine person of all the persons of our heart. The listening of the child of our heart for the sound of God is entirely clear; and the child of our heart is close to the touch of God, and in innocent utter gratitude touches the touch of God and is lifted up and sings. It is like the finger of Adam touching and touched by the finger of God, in Michelangelo's picture of creation.

This child of our heart lives with us in all our ages, and even though we are often blind and cruel in our shutting of him away, so sweet and strong, so tender and generous is this radiant child that he will again and again lift up his grateful heart in song of joy, in song of truth; and he will return us, from the breaks of darkness and the wilds of grief, and even at the verge of death— return us to wholeness, to the peace and the glory he has nurtured within us since the first morning of our becoming.

This little child of our heart is the image of God, formed of light.

7 ✖ *Children of Light*

Question and Story

Do you know the little boys who are the sons of God all about the world?

And do you know the little girls who are the mothers of people of all the world?

The child of the heart of a man and the child of the heart of a woman are both children of light in the image of God but are not entirely like one another. There is a profound religious difference between them.

We stress today that the difference between man and woman is physiological, sexual, as it merely seems to be among rabbits, scorpions, whales of the sea, and eagles on lofty streams of air beside a mountain; and we seem to have forgotten and we scarcely apprehend what every day of life tells us anew that the child of the heart of a man is a son of God and the child of the heart of a woman is a mother of people, which is a profound difference in the poetry of the soul and the religion of the heart, so that the true meeting of man and woman is an antiphonal song of God, and not a carnal fusion. Our tawdry modern doting on sex—quick, to the soonest bed!—is an erotic rotting of gratitude that makes a travesty of love, a travesty of the wonder and joy of love that waits only upon our gratitude to be born in the great antiphonal song of man and woman, which no other creature on earth knows or sings. Our gratitude should be very great, each for the other, woman and man, in the lovely singing of the mother of people with the son of God, and in the presence of God: the deepest of our human songs unto one another, that slowly comes and lasts as long as the heart shall sing.

Let us look at what we are, not in the mirrors of physiology or in the concepts of psychology or in the Narcissus pool of self adoring itself, but in the eyes of children of light and of song.

Have you seen a little Indian boy stand alone, grave and stolid, with the light of heaven upon his solemn face, the while he watches the measuring and making of light across the pueblo walls, across the fields, following its flash over the prancing horses, and its ride up the slopes of the hills, and its return to the mountaintops and the sky? So I saw a son of God in Taos and was touched with wonder. Have you seen a little boy in Spain, where the Guadarrama rises in broken rock to snow and the plain stretches in sunlight from Escorial to Madrid, sit arms about his knees upon a knoll and stare at a drowsing bull on another knoll fifty feet away, and between them in far landscape you could see the mass and towers of a church and the mass and towering of a mountain? The child in the heart of El Greco saw Toledo in storm as no child in the heart of a woman could ever see it. What woman ever lived who could see and paint herself as Job, child of God, with all the grief of God written in the moil of her face, as the unflinching son of God in Rembrandt saw and painted Rembrandt grown old in depth of human pain, companioning God all mortal life long? What woman could ever see and paint the strange tender smile of the child of her heart, as Leonardo revealed Mona Lisa's smile? Have you seen a little boy at a jungle stream in Salvador, where woman and girls with sunshine glowing on their breasts washed and spread out clothes, a little boy crouched at the streamside drawing the pictures of prophecy and revelation with one stone on another stone?

When I was a child in the days of my father's death, and he knew he was dying but I did not, I walked with my father one night on the streets of Santa Fe; and a little boy I knew was dead, and I clasped my father's hand, and looked up at him and at the stars, and I asked:

"Is it true that stars are for dead people? A star up there for each one who is dead?"

And he stopped his step and grasped my hand harder and looked up at the stars in the sky, and slowly said:

"You may think of it that way, child. And be not afraid. For each one of us must die."

And I knew by the stillness in which we stood, and by the hard grip of his hand all around my hand, and by the strange deep of his voice, that he was telling me something profound between us about the death of man, and my death and his death, his all too soon. And no woman could have told me that, for a woman does not show a child the mouth of the adder of death.

And it was my grandfather, later, pacing round and round the dining-room table, with flashes of sunlight coming through the tall window onto his hands and face, with tears in his blue and childlike eyes, weeping and beating his hands together for the death of his son, my father, who told me the word "God," as it is in the heart of a man who weeps and beats his hands in grief, and still trusts God as a little child. And no woman could have told me that. For a woman would have comforted me in her immediate compassion and warm hold of her arms; but my grandfather rendered himself and me to the mystery of God.

And I remember another grandson and grandfather. It was a barefoot Indian child and his barefoot grandfather, from out of the jungles of Colombia, coming to me in their worn white cotton garb, with green jungle stain and brown earth dust upon them, and offering to me the skin of a boa constrictor they had killed in the forest, grandson and grandfather, killers of a serpent of evil, in the primitive mystery of unknowing in which man makes images of evil. And I brought the skin of the great snake back over ocean, myself primitive and unknowing, and gave it to my son, who was then a child, and it still hangs in the room of his boyhood, a symbol of the way of the sons of God—as old as Greece and Egypt and India—that they shall deal with the serpent of life in the jungle of night and the passions of unknowing. And no woman would give a child such a symbol as that; and I would not have given it to one of my daughters; but for them I brought home garments of silk and little figures of people to love.

And when, soon after my father's death, I met my mother crying in the breaks of darkness and the wilds of grief, I did not tell her what my father had said to me, though I cherished his word: "Be and there, she made a very little smile. There is something about the very little smile of these small mothers of the people of earth, the way it almost forms, the way it almost lingers, the way it trusts and accepts, the way it asks for nothing but gives blessing of entire life, that so far exceeds my knowing of human grief and patience and gratitude that my heart weeps, for I do not know how to bless this child before my face. All I could say to this child that morning in Morelia, in the green and golden light below the trees, was the good word of peace of her own people:

"Adios, muchacha."

She seemed to understand that the child of my heart had spoken to her true "God be with you" of communion. She gave the baby a hitch against her side, brushed some stringy hair away from her eyes, still with that smile, as old as the smile of the Mother of Christ, or the almost smile of Niobe, of Demeter, and the smile that Leonardo saw in Mona Lisa's face; and she politely said:

"Adios, señor."

And for that moment the child in the heart of a man and the child in the heart of a woman met with God; and there was an inexpressible warmth of heart and depth of trust between us, a mystery of a touch of God.

And gratitude was a blessing in our two human hearts, hers and mine, in the golden light of the green trees, in one of the old towns of man on earth.

9 ❧ *Joy Toward the Moon*

A Parable

The child of my heart wants to be friends with earth and people and God in sweet delight and living song of gratitude. Being friends with the cosmos is a problem that cannot be solved, only lived. Being friends with a mouse or a man is the same. I cannot solve the problem of my life, but only live it. I think it is the same

not afraid. Each one of us must die." I said, as well as my life could say it, this, that I remember now in song:

> I met thee, caught of fear, bereft of song,
> Eyes hurt, on path of terror, dark and bright;
> Implored thou me: "What shall I do?—so long
> Afeared in cross and cross of tragic light!"

> Thyself was song, where the dark wind blows,
>   And all thy grace shone clear and near;
> I spoke a word love instant knows:
>   "I am thy son. I hold thee dear."

So it is that the child in the heart of a man deals with the serpent of life and the bread of God; and the child in the heart of a woman is mother of people of earth.

And always the mother of the people of earth shall be amazed and startled, and will scold a little, when the son of man dances in sheer joy before the Ark of the Lord. And he will not quite know why hers is always a cradle song.

But in gratitude their song together is music of God.

Man and woman, our song of gratitude together is music of God.

8 ❧ *Mothers of People*

A Story

One of the most grateful things that ever happened to me in these late years of my life was a return to simple children of simple people living life of earth on earth in Mexico.

I came down, a very modern man, in a bird of metal and fire from the sky, heart dulled by the scolding and slaughtering among nations. I was flying with a friend of mine, in his small plane, down along the wild and lovely mountain drifts of Mexico, southward and southward, and from Pacific Ocean to Atlantic Sea. And it was good to land on dusty airfields, to step down onto the ground, and to meet with men and women and children, burros, dogs and cats, to touch finger to a lizard and chatter with a parrot. And in the towns of Mexico, as it were out of my childhood, I was at home, for it was the Indian and the Mexican who sat on the doorstep of my childhood, and several times in the years between I had returned to them, as it were a return from an alienation in a society of artifact, scolding, and war, to the hearth and home of brown and patient hands loving the things they touch, sweet in their sudden joy and learned in sorrow of God. It was not romantic, but very real, for here on the ground of my childhood again I had dealings with children.

I dealt with a little boy on a steep street in Taxco, who was very like a little boy I had dealt with thirty years before, high in a mining village in Zacatecas. In Taxco the little boy had a great basket-weave tray of bread on his head, wearing it like a hat, on his way to market; and bread made by the hands of a mother and given to a seven-year-old son to sell for the family needs is very real daily bread of life. I bought of his bread to eat, and we traded one with another the smile, the word, and the knowing of men about the streets of the world and the depth of the sky. The other little boy, thirty years before, and he was not even five years old, used to come into my patio at the mine and look up at me with trust as we talked a while, and I would give him a warm coin from my pocket, he would grasp it in his little brown palm, and go off singing, always the same refrain: "*Voy a comprar pan!*—I go to buy bread, I go to buy bread!" For they had not much to eat at home, where a sow and piglets lived beside him on the floor; and he took the bread home to share with others.

But it was the little girls who were the most real and the most terrible of all. I had known them in Santa Fe as a child myself; I had known them thirty years ago on the streets of Orizaba and Colima, of Mexico City and Sombrerete; I had met them on roads and entered low doors of houses where they lived; I had seen their

sisters betimes in other cities of the world, in Granad[a] in Tangier and Fez, in the mountains of the Riff and [in] Paris and Rome; and now I saw them again in He[rmosillo?] Culiacan, in Morelia, Iguala and Oaxaca, as well as i[n] Mazatlán. How terrible is the wisdom of little girls [born] of earth! One in a dark doorway in Perugia, with sh[y] eyes and a baby on her lap; and one by a watering [place on a] sun-dazzled farm in Kansas, with sun on her mouth a[nd on] her hip! How profound and tender their suffering is[, these] children of light who are mothers of people!

I met with another one of them in the morning in [?]. It was during the feast days just before Christmas, and [they] were bearing loads on their heads into market, man [and beast] with burdens to barter and share, and boys with burd[ens] and trade. Big straw hats and red serapes and quick [bare] feet. I was sitting on the stone balustrade of a bridge [over the] road, under the green and golden light of large old [trees,] sitting there simply to be there. The air was redolent w[ith] life, of dust, of trees and water. The little girl came, pe[rhaps?] years old, surely not nine, bare of foot, dirty spindle l[egs, a] dress, black stringy hair, carrying against her hip in the[?] dirty shawl the living burden of a naked child half [as big as] herself, a sore-eyed baby with sores on its leg: a vi[llage of] people cherishing a child of God. She stopped to gaz[e at me] with a curious wonder. There was nothing frightened [in her] dark steady eyes and her sorrowed face, but only th[e?] wisdom and patience of little girls who are rooted [in the im-] mediacy of life, who sleep in dark crowded rooms and [know the] smell, the sound, the rhythm of the folk life of passio[n, who are] of earth, of fundamental mankind, and who, as soon [as they are] strong enough, carry about the newest baby of the fami[ly into] the world a while, perhaps until it dies of disease or in[fection,] until the next one comes. Or until, so very soon, the ba[by is one] of her own. When this little girl had seen enough of m[e, of] me, a lean man taller than her own people, but a ma[n?]

for each other one of us. But other persons in the family of our heart do face and deal with soluble problems, such as how to bake a cherry pie or send a rocket to the moon. I think because in our age our scientific intelligence solves so many both gross and exquisite problems of space, time, matter, and energy—which are the elements to be dealt with in making our cherry pie or sending our rocket to the moon—I think because we have learned to cook so well and to rocket so well, we have gone quite mad in the delusion that we can solve our problem of life, too, by instrument and formula. A three-point program for gratitude? A five-point program for love? How silly this sounds, when we ask it flatly where the meaning is!

Perhaps a sort of parable of modern man and the moon, and the child of my heart and the moon, will make it clear that the problem of use may be solved, while the problem of life may only be lived.

Our Russian brothers, employing all the skills of those persons of the heart concerned with problems of use, have launched a rocket that has reached the moon. I know not how many thousands of generations of men have gazed up at the moon and had their thoughts about it. There must have been some in every generation who wished they could reach out their hand and take a pinch of moon-dust to put in their pocket for use of their own, while some others only wanted to talk to the moon and be her friend. To put a pinch of moon-dust in your pocket would be for power, dominion, and doing; and to sing a little song to the moon would be a gratitude of giving.

Well, now our Russian brothers, with the help of many before them and many beside them, have solved a host of space, time, matter, and energy problems—problems in mathematics, astronomy, ballistics, fuels, alloys, rocket shape and design, and so on—and have sent a rocket to touch the moon. This is the first half of the problem solved of getting a pinch of moon-dust for use and power. The artificial and instrumental finger of man has at last reached out and touched the moon. Maybe man can yet solve a going to the moon by instrument and return by instrument, with a handful of moon-dust brought back to give new status of power to states and dominions. Our Russian brothers did as we would have done, with this in mind: they sent emblems of their dominion in their rocket to the moon. This is not making friends with the moon, any more than a prospector, staking out a claim, is making friends with a vein of ore: "This," he claims, "is mine, for all I can get out of it." It is Columbus claiming the Indies for the King and Queen of Spain, for the use and power of Spain. Ferdinand and Isabella soon learned that the wonderful wealth and use and power brought home by Columbus in a pocketful of dust of the Indies did not solve, but deepened, the problem of living, and by the time of their grandson, Philip, the use and power of the Indies had begun to ruin Spain with power and wealth. Moon-dust could be the same. Living by the dream of power often turns into killing business.

A while ago, when I was a man nearly fifty years old, all of a sudden, in a certain way, I saw the moon in the evening sky: and the child of my heart wakened in grateful joy to live the problem of being friends with the moon. There is no solution to this problem, but only a living of it. Compared with the piles of blueprints, the mining, the manufacturing, the ordering of labor, the gathering and spending of money, the secrecy, the calculation, the brain-straining, the propaganda and alienation from others, and such other many things involved in touching the moon with a rocket, the living of my problem of being friends with the moon was only a moment of gratitude, a dance of life in my body, and a giving of word in song of heart. It was only this:

> I was astonished when I saw the moon
> That I have seen so many times before;
> I was delighted when I saw the moon
>   Shining at my door.
>
> Bare trees must be accustomed
> To her silent light;

They do not stir astonished,
  Nor bow delight.

My bow is slender
To a moon so tender.

I could not solve the problem of my life, to live in sweet delight with earth and people and God, in grateful friendliness with all the cosmos; but I lived that moment of gratitude and evensong; and the moon has ever since been a more lovely companion of all my life, because I gave her dance of my life and song of my heart.

We learn these things from one another, by gift of gratitude to one another, child of heart to child of heart. Who first taught my life to dance in joy before great mountains, I do not remember; but it was my wife who taught me to bow to the moon and all the stars, and the singing child of her heart has given the grateful child of my heart song to find the cosmos my more gracious home, from the Pleiades in the sky to the daffodils in the orchard.

We cannot solve the problem of our life, but only live it in grateful song with one another.

I cannot make peace with any man or any woman or any child, but only live it. And gratitude is the first blessing which enables me to begin to live peace with another.

Men and nations cannot make peace with one another, as if it were a machine of politics, of science, of law, of thought; they can only live peace, beginning in the mystery of gratitude.

10 🌿 *Communion in Responsible Tenderness*

An Essay

How do we really speak to one another? So that we really hear and are truly heard, and are grateful in communion?

Whether we say them or write them or sing them, we speak in

more than words. A postcard came to us from Athens the other day. It was more than words. It was an act of life, given to us in trust by a friend.

Is it not true that we speak, that we write, that we sing—or make a gesture, or pause in stillness—always in a frame of reference to our whole posture of life? Is it not true that another person speaks to us in a tone of life composed of the way of his body, the rhythm of his breath, the tune of his voice, the sort of light that comes and goes across his face, and all this imbued with the very weather of his soul? And true that this speech is really what he has to say to us, more revealing and more moving than the mere actual words he utters? So that listening to another person is like listening with your heart to a child, before he knows enough words, as he tells you his joy and his need, his chasing adown of the daffodils or his need of your warmth of heart; or like listening to a poem that tells you more than only its words could tell—as I learned to listen to the poems of William Blake:

> Fashioned from the nimbus
>   Of a new bright star,
> Singing songs no evil
>   May touch or mar;
>
> Songs that fill the stillness
>   Around each word
> With music one who hears them
>   Has not quite heard.

So that the child in the heart of one of us listens to the child in the heart of the other of us, and the child of our heart answers in song of heart. Isn't this the real conversation of human life, the language we most want to speak and most want to have heard, the one we most want to hear and understand from the other? Is it not the language of trust, communion, and peace between us? I know this is the language most grateful to my heart to be able to hear, to try to speak.

It is the word and bread of life between myself and every other one.

This is the dialogue of whole and hallowed life, by which we give and receive life between us.

This is communion in responsible tenderness.

But how hard it is for me, no more and no less than a man, to open and entrust my heart to communion with another, to respond with my life to the trust of another, and to find the fearless strength to be tender!

And yet I have been lifted up by the healing and creative wonder of gratitude—our mysterious consonance with God—to do all these things; gratitude, our first blessing, has lifted me up to do all these things, and sometimes it has led me on also into new wonders of the suffering and the joy of incomprehensible love.

Surely my love of God, which is my most perilous wound and my most infinite communion in responsible tenderness, and without which I could not enter into peace and communion with any other living thing—for each living thing is also utterly of God— surely my love of God began in the first blessing of gratitude.

11 ❧ *Joy, Despair, and Reconciliation*

Theme and Song

The gratitude of a child is innocent, but we know from our days and our years that not all of mortal living is lyric of pure delight. In the paces of time and the throes of life, the innocence of a child suffers mortal bruise in the shock of evil; and then it is hard to be grateful again until we have matured in the full catharsis of tragedy. We may say: The child's gratitude is of innocence; the mature man's gratitude is of reconciliation.

Let these be among the themes for praise of gratitude:

How sings the lyric child of the heart, in innocent joy of gratitude for the touch of life?

How sings an injured man, in dark night of soul, even in anger against the bruise of life?

And how sings the tragic man of heart, reconciled in mystery of unknowing, in gratitude for lived life?

The innocent child of the heart, in gratitude, sings joyful courtesy to earth and man and all the stars and God in a thousand little songs. As we grow older and approach the beatitude of a lived life, we know we have sung many a song of sudden delight in the gay music of the child of our heart, rejoicing in music out of earth— the petal of a flower, the aurora borealis, the song of a bird. And suddenly again, today or tomorrow, we hear it again and respond anew. This morning it is the cherry tree in full pure bloom outside my window, and the blossoms shine against a sky so tender, blue, and bright.

The child of my heart, in joy of innocent gratitude, has sung many a song of delight in companionship:

> Come meet me, my love, where the woodland pond
>   Lies frozen and sheen and still,
> At a moment before or after
>   The sun falls back of the hill.
>
> The trees trace an intricate wonder
>   Against the warmth of the sky,
> And the breeze is laden with color;
>   Through the woodland, shadows ply.
>
> Now, now is the hour to join our hands,
>   And cross and circle the pond;
> We'll draw on the ice swift motions of life
>   That measure a life beyond.
>
> All, all illusions of bondage
>   We'll scatter behind in a trice,
> To rejoice in the freedom and laughter,
>   Embracing the sweep of the ice.

We'll pause at the moment of darkness
  To kiss as a joyous rite;
Then laugh at the star of evening;
  Then skate till the deep of night.

The song of child to child in our human hearts renews us to gratitude and joy of the world.

The songs of a man's dark night of the soul are many, and some are bitter in unyielding despair. What human being could truly say that he was grateful and lived entirely in holy response to the abundance of God through his livelong life? Even, through one livelong day? In the hour of gratitude it never occurs to us not to rejoice and to love. But in the livelong life, I, too, like any man, black my heart in recoil of pain and mutter misery in the sun. And in the marvel of the dark night of soul, when the stars reel and the mad moon leaps at black tormented clouds, does not our heart howl out a hellish word? Bleak, miserable, and mean is a man in his any hour of ingratitude, abusing all his powers to a horrid end. And the hour perhaps most damned of all is the weary desert death in the heart of no response to anything. "Tomorrow, and tomorrow, and tomorrow, creeps in this petty pace from day to day. . . ." But even to a man in this low estate of misery and pain the way of mending in gratitude is open by the gate of prayer. And a man may sing, may pray.

His Song
Fear is falling shadow
  More dreadful than the night
That falls upon the meadow
  From stellar height.

Grief is something other,—
  Hollow, hollow kind:
Fear and grief together
  Torture mind.

His Prayer

Solace, come of praying!
Deep and unaware;
Mind through heart amending:
God is here!

And how sings tragic man, reconciled in mystery of unknowing? He sings in the deep voice of the great poets, Aeschylus and Sophocles, Dante, Shakespeare, and Milton. It is the whole song of the *Antigone* of Sophocles, and is Milton's great hymn—"Hail, Holy Light!" in *Paradise Lost;* and sings in the great Passions of Bach and in the Missa Solemnis of Beethoven; and it sings in stone in Michelangelo's Pietà and in color in old Rembrandt's portrait of himself alive. These things speak to us, from man who has wept to man who has wept.

And one of us may sing:

Here is the simple word of my given life,
Wrought in the joy and loss of love and pain,
Wrung from fall and failure, full steeped in strife,
As terrible as fire, and as soft as rain;
A word hard hammered on the evil stone
Of fear and passion at the heart of hell,
But tender with rejoicing of my love and bone,—
Made holy by the grief in which we dwell;
It is the word I offer to thy soul,
As real as rest, as sure as healing song:—
Let thy receiving make my giving whole,
In mutual trust by which we both grow strong:
    Ask my word for all there is of me,
    As thou I ask thy simple word of thee.

For to know the agony of our life, and to weep, and to pray, and to become reconciled, turns us in compassionate gratitude toward each one we love, and toward this stranger coming near. And he who comes, or she who comes, all bereft of song, into the grace of gratitude our own trial has won, shall be the newest one we love, the newest one we welcome and help in gratitude.

12 ❧ *The Voices of Old*

A Thanksgiving

I am thankful for the voices of old, speaking their deep gift of heart, out of the generations of man, for each of us needs companionship with grateful wisdom in other human hearts.

How nobly it has all been said in olden times, and still resounds in wonderful music of words, in the great voices of the Bible!

And the child in the heart of a man spoke gratitude to God, saying: "How beautiful upon the mountains are the feet of him who brings good tidings!" And also rejoiced and said: "Peace on earth, good will toward men. . . . I bring you glad tidings of great joy. . . ."

And it was also said, to be remembered as long as the heart shall sing:

"Suffer the little children to come unto me, and forbid them not. For of such is the kingdom of God. Verily, I say unto you, 'Whosoever shall not receive the kingdom of God as a little child, he shall not enter therein.' "

And further said: "And a little child shall lead them."

But in the shock of evil, David, the man of mortal pain, cried out in the suffering of the dark night of his soul: "My God, my God! Why hast Thou forsaken me!" And the man of immortal pain, Christ on the Cross, cried out the same words of dark night of soul again: "My God, my God! Why hast Thou forsaken me!"

And the innocent child of the heart and the tragic man of the heart, harmonious in wholeness of heart, sang the whole lovely song of gratitude. The roots of the song are in the Twenty-Second Psalm, where the Psalmist is delivered unto the dust of death but nevertheless praises his Creator; and the tree of the song in its great growing is in the One Hundred and Thirty-Ninth Psalm, wherein the Psalmist is utterly searched out by God, and out of the deep creation of the root and the tree comes the beautiful flowering of full human gratitude in the Twenty-Third Psalm:

The lord is my shepherd, I shall not want.

He maketh me to lie down in green pastures; he leadeth me beside still waters.

He restoreth my soul: he leadeth me in paths of righteousness for his name's sake.

Yea, though I walk through the valley of the shadow of death, I will fear no evil: for thou art with me; thy rod and thy staff they comfort me.

Thou preparest a table before me in the presence of mine enemies: thou anointest my head with oil; my cup runneth over.

Surely goodness and mercy shall follow me all the days of my life: and I will dwell in the house of the Lord forever.

And I am thankful for the deep root of mortal suffering and the strong tree of Immortal Presence bringing this lovely song to flower. For wholeness of gratitude in wholeness of heart is the sacred ground of our joy and our healing and our song.

How shall the heart of a man be great enough to rejoice in his gratitude for the abundance of God? How shall the voice of a man be tender enough to sing of his consonance with God?

Book Two

Earth and Creatures

1 🌿 Earth Wins the Heart

A Song of Life

When I have crossed a bridge in fog-bound poise,
To help bulk and bulk of factories provoke
Their strong machinery to iron noise,
And fed the tapered chimneys spewing smoke,
Or dodged black cranes up-piling blacker coal,
Or helped loud massive trucks consume the road,
Or steered some brutish engine's onward roll,
Or felt a red barge wallow with its load;
Then I have been bereft of natural mirth,
Been stirred to yield to fire, steel, and stone,
Removed from swelling fields of ancient earth,
By love and contemplation left alone:
    Machinery shall bruise and tear in vain,—
    Earth wins the wild heart back to life again.

2 🌿 Praise of Gratitude

Sayings of the Heart

Gratitude arises in the vivid tension of relation and response, in our direct communion with reality.

Gratitude comes out of hallowing and being hallowed, a joy of meeting and knowing, of trust and reconciliation.

Gratitude is our confidence in being, centered in true reality, turned toward God.

Gratitude lifts us up to unity, identity, wholeness, and communion.

Gratitude is the open release in the heart of the affirmation of humility.

Gratitude recovers our life from the torn and the lost, our life offered to us continually by God in the perpetual abundance of reality; and the humble joy of gratitude returns us to living communion.

Gratitude is the rock of the soul in the storm of chaos.

Gratitude is the true direction of the heart.

Gratitude enables us to give the full rejoicing plunge of our life into the oncoming surges of new being, and we hazard our soul with delight to new becoming in consonance and communion with reality, with the abundance of God.

Gratitude is the confirmation and release of our fathomless impulse to generosity. The touch of God comes to us sometimes at a time when it seems not possible to respond with easy grace. Our prudence warns us to avoid the hazards of involvement, and our fear foretells that we shall be found out in communion; and we hide, and hide away from the grace of the touch of God. Gratitude shatters these restrictive contingencies of time and space, these chillings of prudence and fear, and in the warm free tides of gratitude the deep generosities of life in our heart waken and sing.

Gratitude is our spiritual home in infinity, and gratitude is our native home here and now on earth in immediate reality.

Gratitude bounds and leaps and laughs for joy.

Gratitude is our sudden surprise and wonder when we enter with a singing heart into the occasions of God that are the streaming of life.

3 Joy in Earth and Creature

Images in Memory and Song

Do you have a heart for the deep joy of communion with earth? Does the eye of your heart behold and cherish the shapes of earth and the sweeps of light that shape all things new in motion and radiance, in shadow and starlight? Does the ear of your heart hear the soft and the strong and the tremendous music of earth, the whisper of weeds, the booming of surf, and the shatter of thunder among crags, and the lovely sounds of creatures of earth, the creeping, the bounding, the flying creatures of earth, in all music of every weather? Does your heart respond to the wonderful fragrance of springtime rain, the moving silence of falling snow; the tender clucking of a grouse to her chicks among the willows, and the gong of a moose across a lake?

I know I have made a thousand songs out of my grateful joy in being a child of earth in communion with earth and creatures of earth. And it is the space and shape and life of earth, wherever I stand on it and of it, for which I am grateful. My memory is peopled with lovely and grateful visions of moments of seeing and hearing, of smelling and touching and tasting, of being a part of all I saw, enriched by the feel and smell of the water, the leaf, the stone, the scale or feather or fur, the taste of the mountain rain and the taste of the salt sea spray. I have been enriched by the kindred touch of being between earth and I, enriched by the kindred pulse of life between creature and I. I do not mean between earth, creature and the small objective "me" of practical affairs, but between them and the whole central mystery of my awakened and responding "I."

I cannot remember any day of my life when I was not at some moment touched to joy and gratitude by some meeting with loveliness of life in earth and creatures of earth; not even when I have gone visiting into regions of grief or of sickness or of anguish has any day failed to touch me with some grateful touch of beauty of earth and creature. I have never had the dreary misfortune to be entirely dead of heart toward our earth and our life for a whole day long.

Of countless images of memory of this, here are a few:

> I walked to see
> A golden tree
> Beneath a sapphire sky:

Adown the breeze
In shining ease
A golden leaf swirled by.

I had the good fortune once to stand in Interlaken and gaze up at Jungfrau, to walk in sunshine all day long in mountain meadows and gaze at Jungfrau, one of the loveliest mountains I ever met. Do you know Jungfrau, so beautiful at dusk, so still at dawn, so lovely in upper light all day long, as pure as cherry blossom white, as mighty as the signature of God endorsed upon the sky? She companions me still.

I tramped still woodland windings
Through the autumn day,
And heard a startled wild deer
Wheel and bound away.

Now that night has fallen
I cannot sleep in bed
For the sound of sere leaves
Crisping in my head.

And some of the meetings that people my heart, rich with the reality of our mortal condition, are in haunting zones of twilight and death:

Among harsh shards of ledge
A sea gull waits alone
At the sea's blue sparkle edge
On a break of ocean stone;

Grey broken wing outspread,
Bare bone showing,
Red sunset on his head
And sea breast glowing:

His gaze holds steadfast seaward
For the dark touch and breath

Of night dark wafting shoreward
Darker wings of death.

And my heart is peopled with a thousand grateful moments of
dwelling in the midst of light and weather on land and at sea:

I

Green was the earth where the Bob White called
His low-high note, and called again:

Twelve mazy streams of wind and light,
Shadowed, circled, shining, fleet,
Sparkled across the bays of wheat
That flowed to woodland left and right.

Green was the wind-wide field of grain,
And the Bob White called and called again.

II

Autumn in the willow,
    Autumn on the hill,
Autumn by the river
    And the old stone mill.

The mist damp glistens
    On the wary walking crow,
And the fence posts slumber
    When the blue birds go.

And then the sudden sunlight,
    Thick as autumn air,
Glows upon a pheasant
    Startled from his lair.

Autumn in the woodland,
    Autumn on the road,

Autumn mists and stillness
And its golden load.

III

There was a day one day at sea which passed
In cloud-spun fire down the bended sky,
While the weight of waters, empurpled, massed,
Swung round the arched horizon heavily;
There was a burning down the splendid West
Of more rare colors than poor words contain,
Till the winds sang day to melodious rest
And wove night waves upon the water plain;
Hung high, hung clear, above the froth comb wave
The mistress of the night wore one smoky cloud,
And shone upon the waters, and shining gave
Her promise that the night is also proud:
    I'll stay for waftage till such smoking light
    Freights my spirit down the streams of night.

Have you never been like the little boy who went dancing and prancing about our orchard the other day, among several thousand daffodils gay in bloom, and shouted: "I'm busy chasing daffodils . . . chasing daffodils!" Which really was to say: "I dance for delight in rollicking joy of all the world!"

I remember a dawn when I lay in a hospital bed, recovering from laceration, contusion, and shock, with my head bandage-swathed to the eyes, and my shoulder and chest sewed up and bandaged. It was a ground-floor ward. I slipped out of bed and walked out of the door onto the lawn. The last wind of night was quieting down among the stars; the tall trees became very still and the grass was sweet in fragrant silence, and a light of beginning day came out of heaven and shone before me upon leaf and tree and upon blade and blade of grass, and a silent and enduring song of gratitude opened my heart with a joy that still lives in me and that calls me again and again to step out on the earth in the mist before dawn to rejoice in the Other Who brings on the day.

4 ❧ *Spruce Tree and Lost Boy*
A Story of Gratitude in Wilderness

I have remembered in gladness for more than forty years an hour of grateful companionship with a lovely spruce tree in mountains far away. I was a boy afoot and awander in the music of forest and mountain steeps, among the far high mountains of Wyoming, where snow lay shining upon the sharp lavender-colored peaks of the Gros Ventre Mountains, and sunshine was golden warm upon forest and flower.

I was a famous individual that day, that hour, as lonely as Shelley's cloud or as alone as the Ancient Mariner in his most accursed hour, thinking myself proud-minded measure of all things, man, the individual apart, with an overweening concept of himself as the lone omnipotent entrepreneur of the universe, a boy drunk on solipsism, which is a vacuity into which horror seeps; and I was busy at the horror, as old as Protagoras and as new as Sartre, of building images within myself, as if a person could be a person as a self alone, and live; and the stronger becomes the illusion of being self alone, the more cruelly is the heart assailed by the thunders of horror that reverberate in the silence of "All alone!" And so I was awander alone high among mountains in a good ripe fever of this megalomania when a wild outbreak of an actual thunderstorm shattered me down to size, from a self-inflated superman to a live and trembling boy. I was caught, as I entered one of those lovely mountain parks, ringed by forest and peak, by the dark splendor of the storm; of course I had not seen it coming, for in the role of the individual a man sees only himself. I had not seen it coming on huge cloud along the aisles of the sky, nor heard the skirts of its wind asweep in the forest, nor smelled its fresh and sudden fragrance enveloping me, for in the role of the individual, man for himself, a man sees and hears and smells only himself.

I was drenched almost at once where I stood among wildflowers and green glistening grass and beside a wet bush of sage brush in which I dangled one hand. The lightning struck so near I could smell its electric fire, and the resounding thunder was terrible. There was I, alone, an individual, in wild chaos, dreaming himself apart from all life and creator of things to come. For some seconds I was terrified, and my heart choked with horror, for self-inflation had emptied me of my own life with which to meet this majesty of Being now magnificently alive all about me. My first response of grateful sanity that began the end of horror was to the rain and the hail. The big cold drops, with now and then a hailstone among them, were beating on my bare head and face and soaking my shirt to the skin, and some of the hailstones hit my face and breast with sharp blows that hurt. All of an instant, I came out of my fatuous idolatry of self alone and saw where I stood, the radiant spread of the mountain park, the dark forest, the crags, the fire-bursting black clouds aswirl, sheets of rain on gusts of gale and hailstones bounding among flowers around my feet.

To stand where I was in the icy pelting of that pitiless storm until a bolt of lightning scorched me where I stood seemed fatal; and I had no doubt now that the finger of man could not push away such a storm, so beyond the measure of man; but worse than standing still in naked exposure would have been to run twenty yards to a tall spruce tree standing out alone, away from the forest, exposed on a little mound in the park, for it was more of a lightning rod than I, and I had seen such trees after the blast and split of lightning had shattered them. I should have run into the forest in search of a cave of stone.

But I saw that tree, dark and beautiful, shake in the torque of the storm; I saw it, I felt its life, I felt its companionship with me in chaos; and I was grateful that I stood in the midst of the storm not alone; I ceased to be an individual apart and loved the tree, now dimmed by gusts of rain, now radiant in flash of lightning and whip of wind. I began to rejoice at the mutual living together in peril of the tree and I in the splendor of storm. My first concern was not to save my life, and all horror had gone out of me. I chose to live it or die it together with the tree. I uttered my decision in actual words aloud: "Here I go, God, over to that tree. The whole thing is Yours, and the tree and I will take it together." I ran to the tree, crowded under its boughs, wet tree and wet boy, living tree and living boy, and all the roundabout peaks grasped in the fury and flash of storm, and the lovely mountain park where the tree and I were alive together the very cup of earth receiving the violence of heaven. The boughs of the tree whipped in the wind, smelled marvelous, soughed in slash of storm, and shone vivid as lightning struck close and the earth and the tree and I were shaken. I felt a tremendous transcendent unity of the high-toppling and lightning-rent towers of the storm over the outreaching wilderness of mountains, a unity reverberant with thunder and strange majesties of light and odors of fire and earth and water and air—such fresh and sudden living air!—and a tree and I, all met with God.

I sat there on the ground with my wet back against the wet trunk of the tree, warm throughout my body with pulsation of life, and with laughter in my heart I rejoiced in the vivid flash and swirl and trundle of the storm. And when it was over, I clasped the trunk of the tree in an embrace of gratitude, breathed its wonderful odors, and said:

"Good tree!"

Then I stepped out from under its boughs into sunshine and brilliant sparse rain; and standing there with one hand moving about to caress and feel the cool and sparkling wetness of one bough of the lovely spruce tree, I said to the All About:

"Thanks, God."

And before I left the park on my forest and stream way back to the ranch, I stood at the edge of the forest and took a long last look at the spruce tree, and my gratitude had become love; and that tree has dwelt beloved in my heart as a friend for more than forty years, for long over half my life.

And the wild glory of the storm could not measure the terrible glory of God.

5 ❦ *Dog and Man*

A Parable of Abounding Joy

A shining large black dog lived with us for many years, from the time he was a puppy until the time he died; he was a noble and amiable and very large black Labrador retriever, and we called him Storm, and on many a day I was grateful to him for his companionship along the roads and across the fields and through the woods. And Storm taught me what is really the joyous, abounding, and sudden release of gratitude. I know there is an accepted physiological symbolism said to represent the attitudes and reactions of the body in the condition of gratitude; it is said to be a bowing to the knees and a lifting of our hands and face in humble meekness to a benefactor, or to the Supreme Benefactor. But if one has lived alert with dogs and children, one knows that this is not a symbol of gratitude at all, but a symbol of longing, of appeal, even of fear, very often humble, but also even humiliated; and I think the theologians and the psychologists overdo it when they say that gratitude is thus. I think they forget the joy of gratitude that they have seen revealed by dogs and children and, perhaps, by sudden leaping of their own hearts.

I would come out of doors in the sun and wind, with my walking stick, and our great good dog, Storm, would come to my feet and sink to his belly on the grass, and look up at me with mute appeal, then rest his chin on my shoe. This was trust and hope and even prayer, but not gratitude. Then I would say: "O.K. Storm, boy. Let's go, brother!" And the great dog would be swept by a tide of gratitude. He would stand up on his hind legs, every inch my equal, put his paws on my shoulders, lick my face, then leap away and bound in joyous circles round about me on the shining lawn, round about the great maple tree, then prance a few yards along the dirt road one way or the other, until I said to him: "Sure, we'll go that way, if you like." Or said, "Come on, this other way."

And in deep and grateful equality of companionship we would go off together, sharing road and fields and woods in fellowship.

And that abounding joy, the leap and dance of all our life, is the real symbol of gratitude, that my good friend Storm taught me in our years together.

I have many grateful memories of Storm, my companion on so many walks, and here is one in a little song about him when he was communing with the weather on an October day:

> Now abounding wind blows under
> The sun-split clouds
> And lifts up dust
> And shakes down leaves.
>
> Now my shining large black dog
> Furls his body in sunlight
> Small against the cold
> On the green-bladed grass.
>
> And when a gust shakes sun-bright blades
> His smooth side quivers
> And he lifts up his head
> To reprove the wind.

Also living with us was a golden kitten, and when Storm lay curled on the porch or the grass, looking about, so alive and shining black, the golden kitten would curl up in the warm hollow between Storm's ribs and hips, and blink and purr and lick a paw, in grateful trust of companionship between the two of them.

Do you know the grateful joy of being accepted as an equal and a companion of a creature of earth? Do you know the gratitude that leaps and bounds and laughs and sings for joy?

6 🐟 *On Going into the City of God*
               A Rhapsody to a Moose in the Willows

There are no barriers to prevent a grateful man from picking up
the bundle of his life and going into the City of God to live. For
the City of God is never closed to a grateful heart.

Some say the City of God is far off and perhaps hereafter, and
not easy to find or enter; and yet all my life I have lived so near
the City of God that I cannot remember a day of my life in which
some one of its innumerable gates did not open to me, and the feet
of my heart entered for at least a moment of refreshing radiance;
and I can remember many days I have spent all day long in the
City of God. It was not far off, it was not hereafter, it was not
hard to find or to enter. I only need to pick up my life, and turn
my face in gratitude, and enter in, for it is always there and open.

One day a young bull moose in the willows was the warder
of one of its shining wilderness gates who welcomed me in. For
part of the City of God is wildernes of our earth. It was a matter
of painting a picture and of death or life and of mountain gran-
deur, and I shall preface my rhapsody to the young bull moose with
a prelude in homage to mountain wilderness.

I have done homage to wilderness in many ways, and one I
much enjoy is to go out where the earth is great and the sky is tall
and there do homage in the quiet of painting a water color to
that aspect of the City of God that there I meet.

I remember a livelong day of such joy among the mesas and
mountains of New Mexico. Before dawn in Santa Fe I got into
a small bus. It was built for fourteen passengers and the driver;
twenty-eight of us got in in the dark. Twenty-seven were workmen
on their way out to Los Alamos to build some buildings in which,
later, the atom bomb would be hatched from the brain of man.
I had been up among those forests as a boy, and among the cliffs
and canyons of the cliff dwellers long ago, but it would have taken

some kind of security clearance papers or other for me to enter now so grimly a City of Man; and I was headed for the City of God, which requires no papers, but only the visa of a grateful heart. A small man crowded in and sat on my lap as we headed out of Santa Fe in the dark, and over the rim at the break of dawn, and down toward the eroded valley of the Rio Grande in early daylight; and much was the mirth and laughter of the twenty-eight of us jammed in the bus under and on top of one another.

I got out at Española, with my paper bag of lunch and my paints, and that day walked about among the mesas fourteen miles, or maybe more, browsing on splendor of earth and mesa and mountain, now and then pausing here or there for an hour of intent homage while I painted a picture, beginning with morning sun on a pink eroded hill at Abiquiu and ending with a sixth picture at evening, back at the Rio Grande, my bare feet dabbling in the water while I painted my love and my remembrance of Mesa Heurfano standing out alone in the river valley (and the picture has been a part of our living room now for eighteen years). Another hangs in my studio, homage to a great mesa up against the sky at high noon that I can only think of as the Cathedral of the Hand of God, and I know I trembled as I painted it, for it was such a splendor risen into the sky before me; I also knew that I stood doing my homage astride of broken rock that was most suitable home for rattlesnakes, so that there was a kind of hazard of life in responding with my life to that I had met. (Some years later one of my daughters came bounding down off that mesa ahead of a thunderstorm, and met a great rattlesnake in her path, and leapt over his startled shape without pausing to be afraid.) And that day's picture of the mountains of my childhood has hung for years in the dining room of Howard and Althea Clark . . . When I got back with all the men in the bus, and we reached Santa Fe after dark, I knew I had lived a wonderful day all day long in the City of God.

This Paradise of lovely wilderness is very great.

There is a great space in Wyoming where mountains rise up and the earth is wild. Down out of Yellowstone comes the high tumbling of the Absaroka Mountains, and three great ranges spread south-southeast of them: the long-flung range of the Wind River Mountains, the massive granite weight of the Gros Ventre Mountains, and the violent upburst of stone out of earth of the Grand Tetons. A man of my family was there a hundred years ago. Captain Raynolds, in 1860, led a small expedition of Army Engineers sent out to explore the then unmapped headwater regions of America's great rivers. He mounted up from the eastern plain into the Wind River Range, and found and named Union Pass, then made his way down among the Gros Ventre Mountains to Jackson Hole and the banks of the Snake River, and stood face to face with the sudden upflung might of the Teton Range. Later men have honored him by naming a mountain in the Teton Range Raynolds Peak; I have seen it from an airplane where it stands, back of Mount Moran and Bivouac Mountain, a massive silence of leaping stone. When I was a boy I walked up out of the Green River Valley into the high places of Union Pass and camped with some older people there among beaver ponds and forest and beside great peaks where three small brooks begin their life and become great rivers into the seas, the Columbia emptying into Puget Sound, the Colorado emptying into the Gulf of Lower California; and the Missouri-Mississippi, flowing into the Gulf of Mexico; and now one of my brothers lives beside Puget Sound, and I have stood on the prow of a ship sailing down out of the mouth of the Mississippi, and I have waded in the Green River near its beginning, seen it as the Colorado from high cliffs of the Grand Canyon, and flown over its deltas in its lazy flow into the Gulf of Lower California. Many are the chords of remembrance and expectation that touch my heart with gratitude when I approach any gate into the wilderness that is also the City of God.

This summer I was in those Wyoming spaces again, at the ranch of two who were instantly my friends, in grateful revisit to spaces of my boyhood, and hearing happily again the voices and the language of people who know the day and the night of wilderness, voices of men and women of my childhood, voices of my trust in life. I fished the streams and rode the trails and many a day painted pictures. And one day I took my wife to see the place I had lived and worked three summers as a boy. It was a spread of sagebrush at the edge of forest in the foothills of the Gros Ventre Mountains, and one could look across and over little grassy hills with aspen trees in groves on them and see the great flight of the Wind River Mountains dappled with snow. No one lived there now, and out on the flat where I had ridden horseback as a boy and had labored many hours building rod upon rod of fence there was a herd of more than a hundred antelope grazing. I took my wife to the edge of the forest, and there, abandoned for years and the roof caved in, stood the walls and doorway and windows of a log cabin that my brother and I had helped build more than forty years ago. And standing by the cabin doorway my wife said:

"What a beautiful place to have lived and worked as a boy."

The forest was steep behind us, and the sky was very great before and above our faces, and we stood together in the City of God, grateful of heart.

This summer we often went from Beaver Valley Ranch, in the Gros Ventre foothills, up to Jackson Hole to visit the Tetons. And there, where we stayed one night, I saw something I wanted to paint, and came back a few days later to paint it. It was a sudden and astonishing view of the greatest of the Tetons, upleapt into the sky, above a low ridge of forest, a foreground slope with a grove of aspens mystically slender and tall, and a meadow grouped with willow bushes.

It is not easy to behold the Grand Tetons, not at all easy to do homage of greeting them in a little picture—they are so great, so sudden, sometimes most terrible, sometimes most spiritual, sometimes grim in awful majesty, sometimes most lovely music out of earth in rising stone and radiant light. I had walked up to one of their waterfalls and had ridden up into one of their canyons. Now I came to partake in that strange happening between man and earth that leaves faint trace of memorial to it in color on paper or canvas or (primitively) on the wall of some cave.

I improvised an easel of three dry willow branches I found, and first penciled my astonishment at the great peak above the forest and the aspen trees and me, and then began to offer the best response I could to color, light, and form and all the vibrant life of majesty there.

I was interrupted by the anxious blare of an automobile horn. Leaving all but my paintbrush behind, I left the willows, crawled through a barbed-wire fence, and went out to the road, to find a woman there in her car with two children. Her brown eyes were deeply concerned, and, when she spoke, her voice was concerned to save my life.

"Do you know," she asked, "that there is a young bull moose and a cow moose watching you? This is the rutting season. That young bull moose is likely to kill you."

I looked where I had been. Not twenty feet from my improvised easel stood a handsome young bull moose, and nearer to the edge of a clump of willows was a cow moose.

The cow was watching the bull and the bull, with a proprietary interest in the whole landscape, was watching us. The woman assured me that a bull moose may get moody and sullen in the rutting season and might well trample me down. I thanked her for quite probably having saved my life; she conveyed a calm sense of a woman's understanding that men and children are forever doing things to get themselves killed and that it is a good thing women are about to pull them out of it.

She drove away and left the wilderness to the moose and to me.

I think I would have undone the woman's good work of saving my life if I had threatened the moose with my paintbrush and headed past his high nose to go pick up my paints and sketch block. It was a good and well-traveled paintbrush that I had had for many years, with which I had done many hours of painting shapes of earth and weathers in skies around home, in New Mexico, in Vermont, in Spain, in El Salvador, and on the island of Nantucket, too. Its sable hairs, damp from my recent work, were now at a nice point, and would have done as well as a feather to tickle the big moose ear nearest to me, about thirty feet away, as we stood in the sun.

I can only think of what followed as a bit of humorous male business between the bull moose and myself. It was apparent that we both meant to stand our ground and face it out for some sort of decision. If he moved to charge, I meant to leap into my near-by automobile and beat it out of there; if I did not charge him with my paintbrush for a lance, perhaps he would give me some grant of wilderness.

It was obvious that he was not going to stand for any inter-ference between him and his mate from any other male, man or beast. Having myself inherited monogamy from a long string of ancestors, I knew just how he felt and had no intention of trifling with his smooth and prancy wench. I gave her a straight good look of Platonic affection; she tossed her head at me and strolled into the willows, leaving Bull Moose and me face to face to work it out.

We worked it out with that magnificent subtlety and swiftness of creature meeting creature in the presence of God. In such a primal matter as this, I am no more intelligent than a moose; in those spaces of God, the sweep of forest and the upsprung gran-deur of titanic mountains, I was not so intelligent as he in what are the true courtesies of the City of God.

It grew upon me standing there face to face with that gorgeous young beast that there were glories of this wilderness of forest and spectacular upburst of stone into the sky that had never been opened to me and that only a great creature of these glories could perhaps open to me.

"How beautiful upon the mountains are the feet of him who brings glad tidings!"

I was being nobly considered by a noble creature of God. He

stood with his noble antlers uplifted in the sun, and his bossy hoofs shining on the grass; and standing there he not only gave into my heart again the life and spaces of wilderness but gave me my own wildness, too, as a creature of earth meeting a fellow creature of earth in the wilds of God.

He was, as I say, more intelligent than I in this primal matter. He knew before I did that we had in our communion arrived at full respect of life in one another, and that communion in life had prevailed over attack and destruction. He gave a delicate and delightful little toss of his high dark head and sun-gilded antlers, toward the willows and the forest and the leaping of mountains, like a gift to me of passage through his gate into the City of God. Then he slowly turned and in stately grace walked into the willows to rejoin his mate, leaving the steps of my heart free to follow him in realms of companionship forever.

And by gratitude of that moment of grace between us, the wildness in my heart is at friends forever with the wildness of his heart; and a glory of wilderness I had not known before now illuminates my knowing.

I will not detract one iota from the wild glory of the moose in the willows, neither will I in false humility deny that in that occasion of God my wildness rose to glory, too, in meeting with the moose; but I will not lie about what a frail and sissy creature is man, civilized man. I did not, like a dreamer or a faddist, strip naked to go live on my soft pink toes with the beaver, the moose, and the bear in the forests and among the crags. My pitiful pelt would not have withstood the first night of frost; and what would have been by bare feet compared to those of an elk or a mountain sheep on the shards of stone and the sheets of glacier? I hung onto my store clothes and reverted further to civilization: I wanted to retrieve my property—paints and block of water-color paper, and unfinished picture. So I became consciously *homo faber,* man maker of things and hanger-on to things he makes. So, not greedily, but (thanks to the moose I knew still was near) with a fearful and bubbling delight of peril, I tiptoed, prance and pause, prance and pause, over to the willows, through the fence, and snatched back my paltry properties.

It is a very human frailty to gather and hang on to properties, to the arrows we make and the shelters we build and the toys of beauty and use that we play with; and it may contribute greatly to our comfort and our survival, particularly now in the human world of intricate and complex artifice—the world of shoes and money, of factories, oil wells, and ships, of powers and claims and counterclaims of nations—that the tool we fabricate today may be on hand to help us tomorrow. But this possible strength in the City of Man is a frailty when we approach the City of God. A sense of property is a discourtesy to God. The desire to have and to hold diminishes our presence in the City of God. To claim anything as all my own is a theft against grace and a loss in gratitude; and had the moose caught me out in this frailty of human stealing he might have changed his mind and tromped me down under his hooves.

I retreated with "my" painting things, a thief from grace. But still, my heart is more wild and alive by gift of the moose. He has made it a little easier for me now and then to forget "my property" and to enter the City of God. I am grateful for the hallowed grace of his gift; and perhaps a little wiser from clearly seeing one of our human ways of stealing from grace, so that when I do steal from grace, I won't lie about it, too.

Nothing in the City of God can be owned by creature, man or nation, for it is the realm of gratitude and communication. There is no having and no holding in our companionship with God, but reality of being and joy of response.

Book Three

Son of Man

1 ❧ The Wonderful Freedom of Human Bondage

An Essay

How grateful to our hearts is the revelation that comes to us sometimes that we are sons and daughters of man and woman, liberated by our birth into the strange and wonderful freedom of human bondage.

It is a common thing to be a member of a family or a group or a tribe or a nation, of a class or an organization, a church or a club, of a money group or a power group or an intellectual group—any sense of being one of a happy few; but all this is proud, exclusive, and restrictive. Now it is becoming too common to lose our identity in the mass; and that is sterile. It is too common to feel ourself an individual, apart, alone, absurd; and that is spiritual dying. But there is a deep joy in any great moment of knowing we are a son of man, a child of the people of earth.

I know there is a grim speaking of fear of human bondage. We can imagine infinitely, but only finitely fulfill. We can imagine love more perfect than we either offer or receive. We can imagine endless tenure in life and strength, but we die. We can imagine peace on earth and good will among men; but we steal, lie, and kill. Sometimes, like Job, we may curse the human bondage of the day we were born. Our fear of human bondage is simply that we would rather be God. This wish is open to our wild imagining, not to our reality. But open to our reality is the deep joy of relation to one another in the great chain of being, in the hallowed human bondage of being a son of man, a child of the people of earth, made of a Maker beyond our knowing.

That we may give is perhaps the greatest freedom and wonder of our human bondage. We are free to give out of our life and

69

heart to others many living gifts of grace: gratitude, tenderness, love, compassion, trust. We cannot realistically command that another give to us any of these gifts; but we are free to give them and free to receive them with a glad heart when another offers them to us.

Of all the freedoms man may dream of and desire and struggle to win—and most of them are dream and desire for power, concealed under the name of freedom—we have already been given by our birth into human bondage the greatest, truest, and most hallowed freedom of all: the freedom to give grace of life to another and the freedom gladly to receive grace of life that another offers to us. This is the one divine freedom by which indeed we live.

2 ❧ Naked Man

A Rhapsody

I rejoice in what we are, from beginning to end of all our lives: naked child and naked woman and naked man alive upon the earth; for it is in the strong and tender beauty of our bodies, and not in our clothes or in the carpentered shells of our buildings, that we are sons and daughters of man and woman among the creatures of earth in the midst of the wild beauties of earth. Our deepest standing is not with our shod foot on the pavements of cities or the floors of a house, but on our bare foot at the edge of the sea or on spongy earth perhaps beside a stream.

In living joy of gratitude, we see mute faces of life in a blade of grass, so majestically formed and tenderly turning in sunlit breath of air; and in a curve of stone, where shadow sleeps, we see the drowsy dreaming of incredible life. We see it in the way of an eagle and in the toil of a worm.

But how beautiful and beloved is the holy presence of life in the face and body of man and woman and child!

How lovely with sudden spontaneous joy of life is a naked child turning and striving in the joy and laughter of play in his mother's arms between her breasts; and how lovely I have seen a naked child, where she had fallen asleep with her face among violets, under a flowering bush, white petals of the bush drifting down upon her cheek and body, and her hair by her ear still moist from the glee of play, and her soft fingers spread in the delicate wilderness of a clump of moss.

How lovely in all her life is a woman in naked beauty, dappled in sun and shadow beside a pool, alert and whistling return delight to a cardinal bird whistling up above her face in a tree! Her feet shine on grass that is lair of salamander and throne of butterfly, on the pathways of turtle and mouse; and the morning music of the waterfall tumbling over a ledge into the pool enchants the fragrant air. She turns her hair in her hand into a knot behind her head, and stands on a stone, all her tender and lovely grace reflected in the shimmering mirror of the pool; and then with joyous arc and spring she dives into the water, and when she comes up her hair is streaming all about her shoulders, and she shakes water from her eyes and shouts and laughs in glory of life, startling the blue dragonflies that pause and dart above the pool. For she is daughter of man and woman, and one of the people of earth.

How beautiful with life is a man, in all his agile naked strength, riding his bare tall horse in the spray and the sun where great waves of the deep-breathing Pacific overtopple and rumble on the shores of Mexico! Broad and vast is the sea, in soft light toward evening; and the great long combers, building to froth and falling, rumble the ceaseless power of ocean; and the froth and the spray beat about the man and the horse. The horse is strong and swift; but the man has swifter intelligence and motion, as he plays, and leaps to the ground and leaps back onto the horse, with late sunrays gleaming along his prancing legs, his belly, his chest, and light shines upon the joy of his laughing and shouting face. He is friend of earth and of sea, naked companion of light and weather, and rider of proud horses, tender, joyful, and strong, the son of man and woman and one of the people of earth.

We are the naked children of sun and soil, of water and leaf and bough, the sons and daughters of man, and the brother and sister of man, and the fathers and mothers of man, and great is the gratitude that releases us into our true being as man.

What a sublime creature of water, earth, and air man is, touched to life by the touch of God!

3 ✎ *Beethoven's Song of Heart*

A Story

The world is too much with us late and soon, as Wordsworth's sonnet grieved a hundred years ago. Not really the world, which is our native home, but worldliness, our servitude to worldliness. Our servitude to the complex and clashing unrealities of our intellectual structures and artificial fabrications is too much with us late and soon; and we have lost Poseidon and his sea, and gods of earth and air; and since Wordsworth's time our servitude to machinery has become more oppressive and sterile, so what we have forgotten the sublime creature of water, earth, and air we are, touched to life by the touch of God.

Revelation of what and who we are may return again at a summer evening concert.

Tanglewood, in the Berkshire Hills in Massachusetts, is a place of peace and lovely light on an August evening. Once Hawthorne lived there, writing tales in curious but sane consciousness of evil, and his friend Melville lived near by, writing *Moby Dick,* massive legend of evil pride. Now it is the summer home of the Boston Symphony Orchestra, and my wife and I went there toward the end of an August day to hear Serge Koussevitzky conduct a performance of Beethoven's Ninth Symphony.

We went early, taking along a picnic supper, and had time to

eat on the lawn and stroll about as evening came upon the hills
and over the lake, and tall trees darkened with thickening dusk.

We live in a world ethic now of competition and war, sub-
scribing more than we realize to the sad primitive theme that
we are all enemies of one another and that the slayer absorbs the
virtue of the slain. Further, we have corrupted the primitive
forthrightness of this ethic, which granted virtue to the enemy,
by a profound mistrust that grants no virtue to the other one,
and this mistrust corrodes also a true affirmative confidence in
ourselves. We are so silly about it that we classify information and
have ceased to trust those who have it and those who offer it. We
have handed over our lives to a belief in secrecy and lies. Information is sane only as something to be shared among men in gratitude
and trust for better living together; but nowadays it is classified
and concealed as a secret weapon for competition, preparation for
war, and for war. Selected men and women among us are marked
as knowing what they cannot tell and dare not share. I enjoy a
story that reveals the absurdity of this: it is told that a certain
High Churchman had two rubber stamps made for use in classify-
ing his papers: *SACRED* and *TOP SACRED*. I, too, have gone
about in these years of strife with clearance papers in my pocket, a
classified man, carrying classified information, entering secret
places and doing secret things; it is not good for heart or soul. It
is a curse upon the truth of the Word, a withering of gratitude
and a destruction of intelligence. Shall Beethoven not be heard,
telling what he knows of earth and man and heaven? Fortunately,
we have not yet gone so far.

Yet in another profoundly dangerous sense we have gone so
far that we can almost not hear Beethoven utter his great song.
It has to break through our heart-rotting mistrust of one another
and of God before we can begin to hear it. In a world society
of reciprocal concealment and exclusion, where often a man may
not sit down with his wife and children and friends and tell them
what he knows or what he is doing, yet where we know destruction
of others and of ourselves is being carefully planned in secret,

dread and mistrust injure all saying and all hearing.

As the evening comes on at Tanglewood, more and more people gather together, stroll about, picnic on the grass, find places to lounge outside the concert shell to hear the music, begin to enter in under the shell if they have tickets for seats. Before the music begins thousands are there. And how well all of us know each other by classification, and separate ourselves from one another, not only by the dollar standard, according to whether we have an expensive box seat under the shell or mere admission to the grounds, but by dress, by manner, by many subtle forms of consciousness of status. Here a boy denouncing all values with beard and scowl, there one of the international set with her pearls, there a lady from Boston who would wear her pearls elsewhere but not here. Some wear tuxedos and mink stoles, and walk in cultured converse, perhaps comparing what they have heard Toscanini do with what they expect this evening to hear Koussevitzky do; others wear shorts and sneakers, lounge together on the grass, as if giving it a try here tonight instead of at Coney Island on the beach. You'll hear a snatch of conversation announcing a professor or a judge or a wealthy sponsor of culture and music; you'll have a friendly word with a simple country girl in white who, because of some divine gift of voice, is soon to be one of the singers in the great choral movement that rises to climax this sublime work of Beethoven; you'll see two young music students sitting on the grass, their backs against a tree, already deep in study of the score. You'll spot a dozen and a dozen categories of man and woman that are not your category. Being myself a writer, I think of Hawthorne every time I am there, and certainly do not feel in tune for communion with a banker or a beau, with a music student or a member of the international set. You look at people, you look past people, you size up people, and, except for the happy chance of now and then coming across an old friend, you almost never meet a person among all those thousands in whom you feel that humanity is affirmed and confirmed in the meeting. The society of man is atomized by classification, category, status. This is

family, clan, class, tribe, with no common spiritual binding releasing you or releasing them into the wonderful human bondage
of being people of earth together. The only things all have together would seem to be the political right to vote and the military
right to support our ethic of competition and war. A roar of
propaganda or a blast of martial music would anneal these
thousands into mob man, mass man, faceless puppet of noise and
passion.

But it is otherwise with Beethoven. Dusk has deepened into
lovely summer darkness, the breeze is soft, the stars are out.
Hundreds have gathered on the grass close up to the open end of
the concert shell, and thousands have found and settled into their
seats under the lights inside the shell. We have ceased the yakety-
yak of telling our status and yelling our status. The orchestra
is assembled on the stage, and the chorus is there; and Koussevitzky, plump of body, and with his warm quick stride, comes to
the podium, bows, and is applauded. His eyes are blue, and all
his body becomes atremble and moist in his fervor of work.

So! You have heard Toscanini "do Beethoven's Ninth." Now
you are about to hear Koussevitzky "do Beethoven's Ninth."
Which do you like the better? How do they compare? Which is
the better orchestra, the better chorus? This is the last high moment
of the atmosphere of sophistication, culture, up-to-date intelligence.
At least it is for me, for I carry a primitive heart. For the man I am
to go hear Beethoven's Ninth Symphony is—if I dare listen!—to
place myself in the peril of God. It is not now a matter of orchestra and chorus, a matter of conductor, a matter of cultural and
intellectual standards. At the first note of music it is Beethoven—
Beethoven, one of the most sublime sons of men, most sublimly
endowed with music of man singing before God, singing of man
on earth in the presence of God; this is the unclassified Word,
utterly and freely given to all other men, through the tremendous
obedient and humble power of a sublime human soul. That has
happened to Beethoven which makes him more devoutly God's
and less passionately his own; there is no competition, there is

no war; there is the rising wonder of new creation. It is the Immortal Word of the Intelligence of Love, uttered through Beethoven, through the musicians, and given to the ear of my heart. And as this great song, sung through one of the most courageous hearts of the sons of man, rings out and rises in passionate splendor through the hundreds of instruments and voices, I am shattered down to size. I am shattered and shaken out of category and profession and status, out of so-called Ivy League middle-class background, out of authorship of mere books; shattered out of all secrecy of information, pride, or power; shattered out of house, out of home, out of clothes, reduced to size as naked man, no more and no less than a son of man, and one of the people of earth. And I am lifted up to glory in a divine spiritual binding of man's transcendent song in the presence of God, rendered intensely, profoundly, healed and unified, the one unique man I am; and yet rendered entirely one of humankind. And the wondrous tide of gratitude floods my whole being, and my heart rejoices in song, singing with all the people of earth, in the touch of life, in the grasp of God.

Do you know this gratitude? What it is to be transformed by the sublime gift of song from another man's heart—Beethoven's heart, or Bach's, or Leonardo's, the heart of Aeschylus or Sophocles, or Cervantes or Shakespeare—transformed from a narrow, greedy, and status-bound predatory mortal into the great spiritual binding, the deep release and generosity of our divine human bondage?

Turn away from the ant, thou too busy sluggard, and open thy heart to the song of man in the presence of God. Be shattered thyself by the outringing of gratitude that makes thee more devoutly God's and less passionately thine own.

4 🙌 *The Sleepers of Oaxaca*

A Story

Revelation of who we are may be given to us far from home, in a strange place, by simple people who are there.

We came to Oaxaca, a city far south in Mexico, by air at Christmastime in 1955. We came by air, in my friend's small airplane, down out of the northward sky; but the people of earth had come in afoot on steep trails down out of the surrounding mountains.

The afternoon before, we had left Mexico City airport to fly to Vera Cruz but had turned back, for, although we could see the lovely white tip of Mount Orizaba clear and pure in the far sky, it rose above a dark moil of cloud, and all the lower mountains were hidden in the spread of a vast storm, one of those storms that shroud the Gulf of Mexico sometimes for days and climb the mountains to the edge of the central plateau. We spent another night in Mexico City, and after lunch the next day, wishing once more to go to Vera Cruz, we found the weather reports not good for small planes without instruments for landing to go that way and so headed south, past the great flanks of Popocatepetl and Ixtaccihuatl, and their summits were being teased by cloudy tatters of the distant storm.

We circled Oaxaca, lovely in its valley, toward sunset, able still to see the dark storm edging the mountains to the east, toward the Gulf; and we landed on the gravel airfield with considerable bounce in the dangerous thrust of a strong crosswind; and many people in white cotton cloth and with tattered serapes came to surround us and look us over and, when we spoke a few words, to welcome us with nod and smile and jest and brighter eye. Some wore huaraches, a flat sole of leather with thongs over the instep, but many were barefoot.

Hundreds of people had come in to the city of Oaxaca from the

hills and mountains all around for the eight or so days of Christmas festival. How shall a man say who they were? Descendants
of the Toltecs, whose ruined temples crown Monte Alban where
it rises above the town? Mixed with Aztecs from the north and
Mayas from the south, and with Spaniards from across the ocean?
Worshipers of idols behind altars, as some sophisticated people
say? I only care to say that they are people of earth, sons and
daughters of man and woman, children of earth and water and
air, with a deeper knowing of the touch of God than I ever met
in the brilliant world of civilized artifact.

Of the many churches in the town, theirs was the Church of
Our Lady of Solitude—La Soledad, they would say—the church
of Guadalupe, the Dark Virgin, the Lady of the People. This is
a large church of warm, tawny, massive stone, with a stone wall
enclosing a wide paved yard, and outside of that a little plaza and
fountain, then broad steps to a street below the churchyard wall.
For six or eight blocks along this street, and on several streets
running off from it, were double lines of temporary booths and
stalls and open places on the cobbles where people sold and
bartered their wares.

My friend and I first came to this street after dark, carrying our
cameras, hoping to get some photographs of the fireworks in the
churchyard. The street was crowded with a slow liveliness of
unhurried people; unhurried because they knew how to take time
to listen to one another, how to make a gesture slowly, arisen
from grace of heart, and how to listen to another's full music of
word before replying in a word that leisure first had warmed in
the breast. In booth after booth lamp or lantern flared, or a little
fire lit up a heap of oranges for sale, or a family sat on the curb
at the corner cooking supper in a pot set on charcoal between
two stones. The people of earth do not rent a villa in advance nor
opt a room in hotels so much alike, but live on the ground as they
come and go and where they happen to be. Home they carry in
their hearts, and live there always, even when, in our modern
political madness, we powerful ones of strangely corrupted good

will thrust them out of their native space in Gaza or in Kashmir
and break their hearts.

The fireworks had already begun when we reached the broad
churchyard, which was crowded with folk all around its edges,
their faces lit up by the flare of pinwheels and Roman candles,
and streams and sprays of various fire. Deep golden tones of
light wavered up and down the massive walls of the church; it
was such a light, mellow and wondrous, yet tragic and strange,
as Rembrandt saw and revealed for us to see, a light upon the
strange living of mortal man. Great towering frames, shaped like
tall fir trees, were cunningly set up with fireworks, fused in se-
quence, so that the lovely bursts and plays of intense and radiant
fire mounted upward into final climax, and the massive side and
front of the church were again and again lit up by flash and wave
of warm wondrous light, and the higher the light played, the
more humble seemed the masses of people at the foot of the walls,
as if mankind had gathered to celebrate our life in grateful joy
at the foot of the temple of God, which rose aloft above our seeing
into reaches of mysterious night.

Those who performed and who watched the spectacle were
astonished and delighted; even my friend and I soon got over
our mechanized greed for taking pictures, and folded away our
cameras, and allowed our hearts to be astonished and delighted.

There was a room in a building that formed part of the churchyard wall where thirty or forty were gathered in the flare of a
gasoline light, their faces tense, while an old lean Indian of
themselves, his face hysteric and his voice fanatic, harangued
them in religious rhodomontade, and they responded with groan
and mutter and body twist. It was the age-old hypnotic con-
fusion of magic with religion, of idolized emotion confused with
the quiet of God, as old as the Bacchae and as new as Hitler.

It was more sane in the church, where, on the broad long stone
floor, bare of any clutter of pews, a few hundred people were
on their knees on the stone, praying with uplifted faces to the
tall black image of Our Lady of Solitude all surrounded by dim-

pling lights, and with banks of votary candles to her left and
her right. There were no priests there, but only people and their
Beloved Lady; there was no formal service going on, but only
stillness of prayer each by each. Their need was only prayer; their
doctrine was only the Mother of God; and their dogma was their
own heart only.

I was ashamed to move around them as one who was not
of them, as one in need of prayer, but too sophisticated to do as
they did on their knees on the stone; I retreated to the darker lofty
backward of the church.

And it was there that I came upon the Sleepers of Oaxaca, and
fear and trembling tremendously took me and shook the roots
of my heart until I wept.

For the people of earth had lain down in trust to sleep in the
temple and presence of God, and I had never known how so
simply as that to lay down my life in the mercy of God.

In the dark vestibules by the main doors of the church and in
deep shadows by the walls at the rear of the church were a
hundred or more of the Sleepers of Oaxaca. There were knots
of people come in from their far places of birth and of life in the
mountains; and now in God's house they lay together in families
or little groups, asleep in silent shadows on the stone floor; some
of them clasped hands as they slept, some of them pillowed one
another; they shared warmth and slumber, and if a father stirred
it was not to waken but to cover his child with part of his blanket.
I knew beyond any telling in words that I was in the presence
of Sleepers in God, and that they had lain down to sleep in His
peace and His presence, with whole trust of whole human life.

I wanted to lie down among them and give myself, as they
had, into God's sleep and to each other, without any reservation
toward each other or toward God. I was not able. I had not the
courage to meet this occasion of God and utterly become one of
the people of earth. I went to a dark place against the wall and
sat on a bench beside the head of a man sleeping there with a small
boy sleeping in his arms; and I tried to pray, but could not, for

what prayer of a man awake could bless the whole trust of these Sleepers in God? I tried not to weep, but tears filled my eyes and all my body shook. I could not pray, for I had nothing to give. But I wept and all my body shook.

And only then did I forget myself and my shame; forget the sickening fear of myself as a well-informed citizen of our civilized world which is, with arrogant intelligence, slaughtering the people of earth to left and right, in massacres of mechanized monstrosity—Hungary, Nagasaki, Rotterdam—with genocide in the jaws of Moloch as hideous goal; forget the queasy horror and degrading shame of being a coward too proud to entrust my heart to God, a man of our time too sophisticated to remember that each of us is holy and is called upon to move and live and speak in a way that is holy. I knew, as many of us know in our hearts, that in our rage to master God we have forgotten gratitude, and are damned. I was too shattered in my cheap intelligent life and too poor in spirit to offer any blessing to the Sleepers of Oaxaca; not a spark plug from an airplane engine, nor a diamond from the Ritz, nor a hydrogen bomb, complete with directions for assembly and use—these riches of our modern intelligence—nor thirty categories of depth psychology, nor thirty points in thirty political programs, could equal the deep and silent riches of their spirit. But the Sleepers of Oaxaca blessed me profoundly; they reached through all fear and shame and horror of my accumulated years as less than one of the people of earth. They trusted God's house as their home; they were very tired and they lay down in His house and slept in His presence. And they broke a hard crust about my soul absenting me from God; they reached the child of my heart with a gift of joy. They set a light of gratitude in the midst of my heart, where still it warms and blesses all my years.

It is a light that reaches back to my birth and encompasses my death to come, a deep illumination of trust in God.

Book Four

I and Thou

Sayings of the Heart

Gratitude is our ground of meeting; there I and Thou are met with God.

Gratitude is the ground of new being. True relationship between man and man is founded in spontaneous mutual gratitude, the original ground of communion between I and Thou; and this gratitude releases powers of renewed life, creative powers to choose to respond and receive, to affirm and confirm one another, to choose to love.

Gratitude is our consonance with reality, enabling us to build our bridges of trust, compassion, and love unto one another.

Gratitude in our own heart turns our life in trust and companionship toward man and woman and child, toward earth and creature and God, and opens us to communion with one another in responsible tenderness.

Gratitude hallows the heart first, and love comes after.

Gratitude is the root of love.

Gratitude is before love and forever during love, and love does not die in the nurture of gratitude.

Gratitude is the true direction of the heart, and without it we cannot love.

Gratitude generates the intelligence of love.

Gratitude opens our freedom to choose to love; to choose to love is to live on the verge of meeting, and gratitude in meeting establishes our love.

Gratitude is our true response to God present between I and Thou in meeting.

Gratitude opens the heart to growing.

Any two who have been so grateful in meeting as to love may ever after say: "Together we planted the root of love in the loam of gratitude for the presence of God between us, and that is immortal—holy."

Gratitude floods our being when a friend removes the thorn of any pain from our heart.

Gratitude releases our heart to surprise and wonder.

Gratitude is the very earth on which the road of love may be built.

Gratitude in another wakens gratitude in me and liberates new creation.

Gratitude liberates us into larger and deeper living in the realms of trust, of compassion, and of love, giving us responsible tenderness for one another.

Gratitude is our greatest strength.

Gratitude is wholeness of response to the surprise of meeting, and hallows moment and event, person and relation.

Gratitude is spirit of life present in time and place; it cannot be preplanned but is readiness to embrace the surprise and wonder of spontaneous reality.

Gratitude is the loam and the seed, and love is the bush and the thorn and the flower.

Gratitude enables us to entrust ourselves to sacred unreserve and truth in communication.

Gratitude places upon what we say or sing or do the joyous seal of our own free, deep peace.

Gratitude teaches us warmth of speech to warmth of heart, which is being friends; and in gratitude it never occurs to us not to love.

Gratitude warms and hallows our profoundest commerce of spirit, one with another, by touch, by glance, by spoken or written word; and communication between us is made sacred.

Gratitude is the soul of our freedom to give.

And gratitude gives life to the thought of man, and gives life to the word of man, and gives life to the work of man, and gives

life to the adventure of man, and gives life to the prayer and
worship of man: and gratitude is the meaning of the life of man.

2 🖎 *Tender Human Communion*

A Rhapsody

Do you know the wind blowing at night among all the stars,
while man and woman are met in sweet embrace of life? Do you
know the waking of dawn and the rise of day, when friend and
friend walk together and talk together? How shall a man sing
his gratitude for the abundance of God asweep with tremendous
uplifting wings between I and Thou entirely alive to one another? How shall the voice of a man be exalted enough and tender
enough to sing this consonance, this consummate reality that is
living touch of God between Thee and Me?

Do you know the music of earth and heaven, when my warmth
of heart speaks to your warmth of heart, and yours to mine? Do
you know the spontaneous eternity, wrapping all your life and
mine about with joy and song, when your life and mine are profoundly met in the sudden illumination of beholding one another
in unreserved trust, with God's legend glowing in our eyes? Or
with God's music in our voice? With God's compassion in our
touch? And all our senses gathered into the living and moving
mystery of God? Do you know the radiance of gratitude risen
in the heart and rejoicing to God that I and Thou have met and He
is with us?

Do you know the hallowed silence that encompasses us in
poise of life when two of us pause together in any place in unreserved and understanding trust toward one another? The joy
of being wanted where you are by who is there, and wanting that
one there? And we are silent in the touch of God and hallowed
in the watch of God. Have you sat on a board fence in sunshine
with another child, barefoot and silent together in joy in the

warm and vibrant presence of all Being, whether an eagle in the sky or a mouse in the grass? And rubbed your heels against the boards of the fence and grinned each to the other? Have you sat with a friend on a log in the forest in quiet and peace of mutual thought, or sat in the firelight of hearth and home with one for years beloved?

Have I not sat on a suitcase in gratitude of peace with one, amid much chatter round about; and leaned shoulder to shoulder with one against a lamppost in the soft surroundings of night; and with another sat on a bench, now silent, now gossiping together of man and God, together in starlight in a city far and strange, hearing music from lighted human places of people we did not know? I leaned with the first mate on the flying bridge of a ship, in silent mutual joy and trust, sharing his watch with him while mist and midnight spread all about us on the sea, and the engines throbbed and the ship held course, and when we spoke the Word between us was larger than words. I have sat together with man and man in pleasure of silence and dialogue, at a meal shared out of boxes, work-stained man and work-stained man breaking bread together on the floor of a great industrial mill reverberant with the powers and fires of machines; so, too, in a great stone quarry and so, too, in deep tunnels of a mine.

Have not I and Thou lain silent side by side together on the midnight earth, in communion of life, tented in the vast embrace of all the stars that sing and burn? Brother and I in the autumn woods on the banks of the Missouri, all night long; wife and children and I in high mountain forest in New Mexico, through the star-spun night; wife and I on the beach of the sea by the resonant trundle of surf in the darkness. And I and one have together watched the dawn, silent on a lake in a canoe, and softly spoken joy of day to each other as it came. And one and I flew together in a small plane into gorgeous light of mountain storm, with fitful gleam of a deep-canyoned river threading its wild gorge below us, until suddenly the storm hid the face of the earth and turned all air black about us, and in a word of companionship we relinquished our will of that day's venture to the stormy mystery of God's might, and turned about to land where we began our flight, to fly another day.

Whose life could not remember and sing a thousand gratitudes such as these?

Do you know the deep release and divine healing of gratitude, illuminating and warming all the reaches of your heart and fulfilling all the yearning wonder of your life, when the touch of your hand, the sound of your word, and the smile of beauty you cannot see on your own lips, in your own eyes, confirms and comforts and loves another human being? And out of the depth of that other heart comes up a light of the presence of God to shine upon you from that other face? I cannot see the radiance of gratitude lighting my own face; but I do know that my heart has leapt for joy and sung for glory in the sweep of this loveliest of human blessings, that gratitude freed me in a moment of spontaneous eternity to give my life to another. And if I wept, it was in tears of peace; for our heart of agony was broken and our heart of peace restored.

Many and many have met with me in gratitude in the years of my life and the days of my doing.

Thou. . .and thou. . .and thou. . .

Have we not taken sweet counsel together and walked toward the house of God?

3   *Our Own Heart Is the Home of Gratitude*

An Essay

Gratitude is not, in its essence, a thing we get from somebody else, like a box of candy, a bunch of roses, or coin of the realm. Gratitude is in essence a revelation that takes place in our heart and makes it whole and unafraid and glad. It is the generous sun of our inborn consonance with God, coming out of eclipse, and first irradiating our whole being with new warmth, and thereby freeing us to pass on our joy in grace to others. This sun shines readily at many times in our lives, particularly when we live and watch and listen and participate in childlike trust; but when the eclipse is long and dark, then warm bright gratitude has to break through the queasy horror darkening our heart and has to clear away the hysteric turmoil that fogs and dizzies our mind.

Gratitude is our free, participating, and joyous release in and response to an occasion of God.

Our own heart is the home of gratitude.

Our own heart is the warm and living home of gratitude, where we welcome one another into all our life in the presence of God. For the son of man hath nowhere to lay his head, until we open our heart in gratitude and give him home. And I and Thou are homeless, too, until we welcome him. Until we welcome this man, this woman, this child into the life of our gratitude, we have no home. I and Thou are homeless until in our own gratitude each of us welcomes the other.

Anyone may be lost and alone when angry and hurt, fragmented and forlorn. But when gratitude opens my heart, or yours, we cannot be alone; God is present, and every other thing is alive with me, and I am alive in life with other being, and very alive with man and woman and child.

In gratitude I am alive with Thee, and my heart is a home to Thee.

4 🥀 *Lovely Moments of Gratitude*

Images of Memory

Lovely moments of gratitude touch our lives and bless us, and leave behind images of memory like little songs of light in the heart.

One that has touched me more often than any other, until it is like a song and symbol of the music and light of gratitude, is a warm, gay, and glowing light on a woman's morning face, when she wakes from sleep at the sound of my voice, and looks up at me standing there, and smiles in gratitude for something between us greater than she and I, for the presence of God. She will call it by other names than the presence of God, as a woman will, for that is a man's way of speaking; but the song and light of the mystery is gratitude.

I have seen a man smile for the presence of God between him and his delighted grandson, seated together on his horse to give the boy a morning ride; and the broad brim of the man's cowboy hat, shading his face in mountain sunlight, could not hide the human beauty of his smile.

One of the loveliest things I have ever seen was a warm shy smile of gratitude lighting up a woman's face in the midst of a cubbyhole cocktail party, where noisy avoidance of life was killing the hour. A shadow of long-endured fear, bleak and cold, haunted her face with torment; her life was suspended a thousand fathoms below the froth of the party; she dwelt bewildered in profound dread. At the sound of a word that was warm, spoken to the child of her heart, a miracle of light came from within her, shattering the shadow of fear on her face. Light of gratitude began to glow in her heart and came up to light her face with tender joy, and her life gave forth warmth of new being. During her moment of gratitude she became one of grace who gave blessing.

We do not worship each other, I and Thou, but God present with us, the touch of God between us; and the smile of gratitude that lifts up our heart and lights our face is of surpassing beauty. And whoever smiles gratitude to God in the presence of another human being has hallowed our human life. And who sees such a smile is blessed by it.

One of the loveliest sounds I have ever heard was the voice of a man saying a few simple words in gratitude. He was a Marine sergeant, and we were in an airplane hangar at an air base. An explosion in my face had knocked me to the floor, and he came running to where I lay sprawled and bright with blood. He knelt by my side and found me alive, and comforted my shoulder with his hand, and in a voice made utterly tender with gratitude that he found me not dead, he said: "You will be all right."

And I was blessed by the depth of gratitude in his voice.

Have you not heard the warm and tender voice of gratitude when a child finds his mother is there, when a woman finds her husband is there, when a man finds his brother is there?

And the touch of gratitude is the most living, sure, and tender touch with which we touch one another; it is the touch of God between I and Thou. I have felt it in the dark of night when I have lifted a child in my arms, and the child, no longer afraid, patted my cheek in tender wonder, peace, and play of gratitude.

This touch is a touch of blessing.

The touch, the word, the smile of gratitude are the blessing of life between us.

When I am grateful myself, or when I meet with gratitude in another, my heart laughs with music.

5 　🖎　*A Man—A Woman—A Child*

Three Songs of Life

I have sung many songs in my life in gratitude for human companionship. Out of such songs that my heart has made in gratitude that I and Thou are met in the watch of God, I now sing three again, first sung long ago, for a man and for a woman and for a child, and the gratitude of these is true of all my gratitude in human companionship.

I sing of gratitude that welcomes companion man, my brother in God, into the home of my heart forever:

　　We rode between two mountains toward the sky
　　And felt the western wind upon our faces;

We slept where sounding waters swirled by
Or built our evening fire in silent places;
We shared the morning cliff and noon-weighed plain,
Smelt sand and grass and windy forest pine,
Or crossed a stream we never crossed again,
Or watched the heavy heron's twilight line
Of flight above a marsh; and sometimes spoke,
And sometimes sped our meaning with our eyes,
And often with a gesture could evoke
Our harmony of venture and surmise:
 We have this treasure until final rest,
 That we were friends and brothers in the West.

I sing of gratitude that welcomes woman, my companion in
God, into the home of my heart forever:

 My wife went in
  Through the old barn door
 And searched around
  The dark barn floor;

 And there among the shadows,
  And there among the trash
 She found an old milk stool
  Fashioned out of ash.

 She brought it in the house
  And washed it clean
 And set it by the fire
  Before the screen.

 Abandoned in a cow stall
  I found another,
 Fashioned out of thick oak,
  The ash stool's brother.

The ash has three legs,
  The oak stands on four,
And they are thrones
  On our parlor floor.

Thrones at our fireside
  (Where the cherry log flares)
Inviting us to sit
  And forget our cares.

We sit there and gossip,
  Chin in hand,
And hear without a shiver
  The wind's demand

As it whistles at our window
  And sighs across the hill,
Then rattles at our shutter
  With thwarted will.

We sit before our fire
  And re-tell our day,
And warmed with a sure warmth
  Re-find our way

Back to the wonder
  That began long ago,
Back to the stillness
  That lovers know.

And I sing of the gratitude that welcomes child, my companion
and ward in God, into the home of my heart forever:

Sleep, my Child in the orchard, sleep
Beneath the moon's sweet eye
And the bat's slant wing;

Dream, my Child in the orchard, dream,
The while I sing,
Slowly sing and gently sing.

Fair stars scarce measure
The soft deep sky,
And dim their treasure
While the moon rides by.

On meadows hover
Mists fresh and still;
Old woods drowse over
Each ancient hill.

Soft winds scarce flutter
Your lock of hair,
While slow boughs utter:
"Thy dreams be fair!"

Once, my little son,
Long ago,
I was a little son,
Sleeping so.

6 ❧ *Three Foremost Things*

An Essay

It is gratitude that enlightens and endows with life the three foremost things that Thou and I may do together.

It is our gratitude for vivid radiance of being that enlightens and endows with life the word we speak to one another, and the work we do in help of one another, and the venture we hazard for and with one another.

Christ did not speak for himself alone; Hercules did not labor for himself alone; Prometheus did not venture for himself alone. Socrates did not speak for himself alone; Lincoln did not labor for himself alone; Columbus did not hazard the ocean seas for himself alone.

And Thou and I, when gratitude lifts us up into life and presence of one another, do not speak alone or work alone or venture into any new being alone.

No man or woman or child can do a foremost thing alone, for in foremost things we are members of one another.

7 🐟 *Hallowing Our Word*

An Essay

Gratitude makes the Word between I and Thou holy. What we sing or say to one another, or our written word, in gratitude has the joyous seal upon it of our own free, deep, and life-giving peace, and communication between us is sacred.

Our word of gratitude bears life; it is the Music of God, given to us, and we may share life between us in its holy meaning. It is gift to one another of trust in life.

Out of the Word that I and Thou share in our meeting in the watch of God stream two great streams of blessing: the blessing of survival and the blessing of illumination—the intelligence of science and the intelligence of love.

Our word of the intelligence of science is a good tool for our survival, Thou and I making bread and raising shelter. By our good use of this word of information we build our great artifices of culture and civilization. Great men like Pasteur have spoken this word of the intelligence of science so truly as to save many thousands of lives. But when the word of the intelligence of science is put to the uses of evil imagination—as I and Thou are doing today when we use it to guide the brilliant fabrication of hydrogen bombs and other tools of genocide—it becomes a word of destruction; destruction within us, destruction between us, and destruction all about us.

And the Word of the Intelligence of Love is a divine mystery of blessing between us. By word of heart, in trust of life, touched of God, I and Thou pass life and increase of life to one another. But evil imagination in the heart turns this word into a lie, and I and Thou slay life between us.

It is by gratitude that the Word of the intelligence of science and the Word of the intelligence of love are kept sane and strong and tender in communion between us, preserving and giving life, and building new creation of life.

8 ❧ *The Word Is of God*

Meditation and Prayer

As a man who has been given gift of word, I am deeply conscious of my need for meditation and prayer in my use of word.

The Word is of God, and I tremble before it. Here am I, a son of man, living at a time when one of the great meanings of human bondage is that I am endowed with the word as a tool of human intelligence made wonderfully subtle and powerful by the sane and patient spiritual labor of thousands of generations of men. It has been given to me in trust by the labor of all our forebears, to use in honor for our life, and to render undespoiled, and by my own honor and labor a little strengthened, to the sons of man who come hereafter. In the aeons of the past, aspiring man had almost no syllable of this cumulative word of intelligence: almost no art, no medicine, no mechanics, no mathematics, no word of science by which to ameliorate the stark challenges of survival, and almost no word of gratitude, trust, and compassion by which to illuminate life for another. Now I am born to prodigious wealth in the accumulated word of human intelligence. Forgotten men spoke the word that brought into our life and hands the knife, the needle, the wheel, the lever, the planting of food, the husbanding of animals, the fashioning of wood and stone and metal. Archimedes and Euclid already received a vast inheritance. And has not Hippocrates, in his oath, taught us how to honor this word of the intelligence of science? For Hippocrates in his oath established that the purpose of science is to save and not to kill. And forgotten men brought to conscious human intelligence the word of trust and of love and of peace, so that long before the time of Moses or Buddha or Socrates or Christ our inheritance in this word was also very great.

The word—call it tool or call it increasing human intelligence of God—my noblest inheritance from the spiritual toil of the people of earth and all the generations of man, comes to me now so brilliant, so subtle, so powerful that I stand in terrible jeopardy of destruction if I dishonor it and debase it to the uses of evil imagination, instead of lifting it up in gratitude toward the giving of life.

I and Thou are met with one another on the pathways of eternity, and all our doing is a moving on the way, and when we ask and tell one another how to do this or that—whether to improve our pleasure or improve our fortune, whether to deepen our trust or open our heart—we are using the word to tell direction to one another toward good or evil, toward life or death.

I tremble with fear of God in the presence of my own evil imagination, for I am a son of man with terrible power to corrupt the word and kill thee. In arrogance of self-will, in thrust of passion, in sloth of ignorance, in the grasp of greed, the evil imagination of my heart could tell thee the turning toward death. I need but put the accent of evil on a syllable here and a syllable there, and I have killed thee.

And so I pray for grace and gratitude to keep this Word holy.

Have you ever prayed that you may be so grateful for this wondrous tool of human intelligence, this increasing revelation of God, that you may use it with all your strength for wisdom and for peace and for life? Do you labor to clear away as well as you can the sludge and dark of your own ignorance, to bridle your furies and temper your fears, so that you may offer the word of practical intelligence and the word of the intelligence of love among men with affirmative grace and healing help? Is this subtle gift and power of your intelligence directed by a grateful heart to the more wholesome and more hallowed living of man?

I tell thee, I must pray again.

I must learn by work of my spirit, before I speak, how to speak.

Each new morning of my life I am in profound need of prayer to learn how, in gratitude, to hallow the word.

Until my heart is established toward truth, I am not worthy to speak.

I pray God to teach me never to trifle with the terrible and beautiful reality of life and of death, which is His Word.

9 ⚜ *The Word of the Intelligence of Love*

An Essay

The word of the intelligence of science, from before Archimedes to after Einstein, is the word of bread alone. And I and Thou do not live by bread alone. For all its sublime utility as a tool of human intelligence for survival—more comfortable and more secure survival—this great word of bread is futile until it is complemented and suffused by the deep word of not-by-bread-alone, the word that rises up from the roots of gratitude, the word of the intelligence of love, become holy by the sweeping through it of the music of God. And survival becomes illuminated life.

I and Thou in gratitude may speak the word of the intelligence of love so that our survival becomes illuminated life. But we must first confess that the intelligence of love sings in a compassionate voice of life too profoundly real to be easily borne by our passionate daily drives of self-for-self.

It is easy to name great souls who have spoken out of their gratitude the word of the intelligence of love, illuminating our human life; but it is not so easy to inherit and speak this grace of word as to inherit and speak the word of practical intelligence. I have learned in a few hours how to understand (for practical purposes) and how to apply in practical work Boyle's Law concerning the pressure and volume of gases; and in a whole lifetime of aspiration I have not yet learned how to understand and apply the word of the intelligence of love as the great and greatest souls have done: "Our Father which art in heaven, hallowed be thy name. . . ." When shall I understand and be able to speak this word that blesses God? But the great souls have been many, and gratitude lifts up my heart toward them to do as well as I am able. David in his psalms was deeply troubled and moved by the intelligence of love; and Socrates spoke this word with a heart serene and a smiling mind; Christ spoke it most deeply of any voice we have ever heard, and St. Francis was sweetly endowed with it; in Dante's song it has a stern justice and sublime vision; it is like broad and fertile day and tragic, mysterious night in Shakespeare; in Erasmus it was reasonable and tolerant, and in Thomas More witty and firm as heart of oak; and in Lincoln the word of the intelligence of love was mystically shadowed by the compassionate grief of God.

Thou and I in gratitude may uniquely learn it and uniquely tell it, each man's song a little different from that of any other man, but divine foundation in gratitude the same.

When my heart is grateful, and by gratitude unafraid and open, I know how this intelligence of love wakens in me, shattering the word of my practical and finite manhood with an illumination beyond anything I ever was or am of and by myself, and breaking my passionate masks of self-for-self with the sudden joy of sacrifice, the joy of that true and liberating sacrifice which is the laying down of the passion of my self and the will of myself, to rise up a person of God and sing. Although in passing through my frail and dense mortality into the word and work I say and do the song is lessened, fragmented, obscured, still it is the word of man touched of God, and bearing life toward another human being. My life stumbles, but Intelligence of Love sweeps through it on transcendent wings. There is a Music out of Earth and Heaven that stirs our mortal dust, and shakes my own. It is not biological love or animal affection (though I am delightedly moved and grateful for them when they are naturally there); but it is a motion of God playing through me like lightning blazing through the heavens. It is always the sweep of transcendent wings and the flash of transcendent light, illuminating my dust with music and liberating song from this mortal coil of flesh. That happens to me which makes me more devoutly God's and less passionately my own. Then all the man I am, of memory, of immediacy, of imagination, becomes servant of the song. And this song which shakes me throughout—this word of man touched of God—is a trouble and a dread to the ordinary prudent mortal in us, and a trouble and a dread to any mortal who hears or sings it, for its call is to the root chords of our life, and it shakes thy whole heart and mine with transcendent tones. I and Thou suffer reality with human pain and joy, broken open by the music of God, when my poor mortality or thine sounds forth divine song, with mortal distortions of that immortal music.

"Hallowed be Thy Name!"

I am grateful for this rending that liberates the word of the son of man, touched of God, among us, in thee or in me, by which word I and Thou pass life and increase of life and deepest meaning of life to one another.

But we are not often or for long in the ecstatic sweep of this divine shattering.

There is a humble common saying of the word of the intelligence of love, spoken between I and Thou in our daily life and doings and sudden joys of heart, for which I am daily grateful.

I am grateful for the word of affirmation given and received between I and Thou, the direct word of a childlike and candid heart, the word of warmth of heart directed to warmth of heart in simple trust of life, saying perhaps simply "hello" or pointing perhaps with joy to something near to both of us: "Now dusk has fallen and the dark and outspread hills lie adrowse, dreaming of the moon. . . ." How lone I am until another voice speaks to me the word that affirms my being, affirms our world; and still how lone I am until I lift up my own voice and speak to Thee a word that affirms Thy being and our world!

"Abide with me. Do you know the wind blowing at night among all the stars? Come, let us rise in the morning and step out on the earth in the mist before dawn, and rejoice in the Other between us, Who brings on the day."

10 🌿 *Word of Man*

A Song of Life

The word is holy.

And the first thing and the great thing in the heart of each of us is that I and Thou want to say and want to hear that which is holy. God has put it into our human heart to love the child in the heart of one another, God gives it to thee and me to rejoice and sing, so that I and Thou may shatter misery by a holy word.

And so I sing again, and every day of my life the deepest prayer of my heart sings again:

> Here is the simple word of my given life,
> Wrought in the joy and loss of love and pain,
> Wrung from fall and failure, full steeped in strife,
> As terrible as fire, and as soft as rain;
> A word hard hammered on the evil stone
> Of fear and passion at the heart of hell,
> But tender with rejoicing of my love and bone,—
> Made holy by the grief in which we dwell;
> It is the word I offer to thy soul,
> As real as rest, as sure as healing song:—
> Let thy receiving make my giving whole,

In mutual trust by which we both grow strong:
　Ask my word for all there is of me,
　As thou I ask thy simple word of thee.

11　✍　*Joy in Our Work*

Question and Song

Have you built a stone of shelter and a window of beauty into the edifice of the son of man on earth? Have you lifted up your heart and put forth the strength of your hand and your soul to help build the cathedral of man, consecrated to God? For this is the work of gratitude, and it is holy work. Have you sharpened your tool with patience, and moved to your work with a quiet joy? Have you beheld true need of another forming the design of your work and asking you to do it well? Have you seen where the labor was large and heavy for one and stepped to his side and said: "Here, let me help you with that"? Have you done true work of a man, that I and Thou need and want and are able to do helping one another?

Our true work is not alone, but work of I and Thou together. And if our word to one another be holy, then the work I and Thou do shall be hallowed in help of one another. It is not secret, it is not classified; it is open, grateful, and good.

Have you labored so that I and Thou may eat? Have you in the limber years of your youth sat on the iron seat of a hay rake, driving a team of roan mares in the thousand-acre meadows of Wyoming, in the blaze and haze of sunlight, with forest fire smoke rising among far mountains, and the timothy ripe and the redtop sweet, and raked up long windrows of hay for your fellow workers to sweep and stack, for the feeding of cattle in winter and the feeding of men in cities? And one of the roan mares had a colt, and the colt broke out of the corral, and came to the whinny of its mother, and got its head twisted in the tugs, seeking milk of its mother, and you had to be gentle to untangle the colt, for a colt has a right to its mother's milk?

Have you labored and sweat in the sun in a great quarry, help-ing another and another to blast and move and grind the stone of cement for the building of houses and roads in a thousand places, and crouched in a great iron pipe when you pushed down the plunger of the switch that dynamited ten thousand tons of stone from the quarry wall, and rock beat upon the pipe and bounced before your face?

Have you helped stir a cake in the kitchen?

Have you sat in an office near the harbor, watching ships go by, out past the Statue of Liberty, and toward the sea, and thought of the life of a ship on far oceans, and turned with new care to your work, which was to write down correctly and rightly tell the officers of the far-flung fleet of oil tankers of new hazards to watch for off the coast of Maine, new lights to look for approaching Galveston, new channel buoys to guide them up the great river to Buenos Aires? And the quick, tall girl in the mimeograph room helped you correct the proof before you sent the word to the seven seas to guide men and ships at labor for the son of man?

Have you climbed and crawled in the sun, laying new shingles on the roof to shelter your wife and children?

Have you heard the question of a student in your class that you could not answer, and heard his need to be answered, and gone home into toil of spirit and seeking and trying to find, and re-turned to class another day and spoken out to the student the best answer your heart could find? And there came upon his face a smile like a light because your labor had answered to his life?

Have you done homage to light and form and beauty, met in loveliness on earth before your face, and painted a picture to rest and delight the heart of another? Perhaps it was a simple tree at evening in El Salvador, with lovers sitting beneath it and a mother and child walking by?

Have you in some instant summoned your skill in care and pre-cision of doing and saved a life or avoided a death? Perhaps it was only that common thing, while driving an automobile on our fast highways, of giving sudden extra measure to your work of driving to make up for blind or stupid work of another driver?

Have you tried to write down a story for others to read and live by, knowing that at the heart of any story you could ever tell in true work would always be the tragic wonder of the human spirit and the greatness of its motion toward God? And of all your books, risen out of gratitude and enriched by all your loves, whether in song or essay or story, one was called this and one was called that; and wasn't each book and each time a making of song between I and Thou? And I could not sing at all, unless first God had made me, and then Thou and Thou and Thou had helped me live.

I have made a sudden song of gratitude for the joy in the long work and the long song of being a son of man in companionate human bondage under God:

> How good it is to be a limber reed,
> Rooted, and wild in sweet responsive flash
> To the divine blowing of our daily need,—
> Rooted in God, and unafraid of brash
> And blowing wondrous winds or sudden light
> That burst like fire and music out of earth,
> And sweep my spirit with new create delight,
> Refreshing every moment with an holy birth!
> O, thus to be a man of earth and God,
> With root in Being, and being formed for song,
> A singing reed upsprung from hallowed Sod,—
> This joy that God began, love long prolong!
>   Sweet glory is it, that a man so springs,
>   Upward grows in radiant light, and sings!

Have you built a stone of shelter and a window of beauty into the edifice of the son of man on earth? Have you lifted up your heart and put forth the strength of your hand and your soul to help build the cathedral of man, consecrated to God? For this is the work of gratitude, and it is holy work.

And I and Thou rejoice in the work of gratitude, by which we help one another.

12 ❧ *Adventure into Mystery*

An Essay

We long to be the first adventurer into new realms. A vain imagination stirs our heart and drives us forth into the dream of being first discoverer, the strongest, wildest, strangest, and most superb. And we commit the sin against life of going alone.

Have you returned from high skies and far seas with a homeless loneliness in your eyes? Have you come down from the mountaintop with cool and windy loneliness in your eyes? Have you regained earthy mortality after soaring in mystic realms, erased of person and set apart from life? Have you come up from the deep abyss of psychic netherworlds of only yourself plunging in the abyss of yourself, alone and haunted by chaotic monsters crowding your hollowed heart? Have you been the first in pride of being first, and the last in gratitude to love?

These are the misadventures of our ingratitude. He who ventures alone shall find no home in the universe. He who sets out to conquer has already lost his home and thrown away the meaning of his life. For the sin against life is to venture alone, wander alone, stay alone.

We dream a solitary greatness for ourself. Our human heart longs for adventure and our imagination shapes marvelous dreams of battle, voyage, and conquest. We shall be the first to find new worlds! We shall keep them for our own! We shall be a cosmic Don Juan and seduce the universe! We shall be Faustus empowered with all power for the mortgage of our soul! Until finally our evil imagination dreams that we shall be God. As mad as Stalin. As insane as Hitler. As crazy as those incredible people—alas, ourselves!—who now make and hold in our hands ready to use the toys of disaster to demolish life on earth. In our ingratitude we have now run mad, seeking misadventure into new horror, the hollow and deathly nightmare of each of us being a lone individual greater than God, and collectives of us crushing the person, the true person of God, out of every heart and life.

Only I and Thou, sealed unto one another in gratitude, can fulfill the great adventure into reality, of meeting and becoming persons in the greatest meaning of life, of becoming I and Thou met with God. This is our true adventure into mystery. How strange to seek the empty misadventures of vainglory, and run from, hide from, miss the adventure of new creation that begins in gratitude with I and Thou now met and here! This adventure of reality and new becoming, this communion between us of unreserved trust in holy speaking, holy working, holy daring, calls upon us for all our humility, all our courage, all our strength of suffering, all our tenderness of compassion and all our rejoicing in gratitude. It is the adventure of communion in building our spiritual home face to face with one another in the presence of God. It is the daily bread, that is not bread alone, of our human heart. It is divine wheat sprung from the loam of gratitude.

And until I and Thou are well met in this only real adventure, there shall be no home and no bread of God for either one of us.

Book Five

Our Time and Place of Life

1 ❧ *Our Time and Place of Life*

Our time of life is now and our place of life is here. When we are not grateful we have no home in time or in place. When we are not grateful we have no home in the presence of God, and cannot love. If we are not grateful here and now, then where shall we go and when shall we be grateful? Where shall we find home and when shall we find home? In infinity and eternity? But they would be neither infinity nor eternity if they did not also completely absorb both here and now. I think we are a little afraid of the tremendous mystery of God that entirely absorbs here and now in infinity and eternity, and we would put off the continual new creation of our life in gratitude until some other time and some other place, more comfortably imagined and less awesomely real.

But we cannot do it, for all our desire and imagining. We make our home in gratitude here or nowhere and now or never. And in spite of the phantasies of the intellect that haunt and lure us toward the illusion of a man-made time and a man-made place of perfect fulfillment—some Utopia of politics, economics, religion, and passion, with science providing the know-how of perfection—most of us find grateful measure and meaning of home here and now in our daily living in our own small parish of love.

I know that gratitude has given me home in a small parish of love since the day of my birth, and that it was always here and now in this humble community of common life that I was real and life was real and gratitude was the first meaning of life. I may differ a little from every other human being who ever lived or ever will live in the design God gave my fingerprint; but it is well for me to remember that a different whorl or delta on my thumb puts me neither above nor below any other man or woman or child, but puts me in the common midst of humanity. And so, as I honestly try to tell what I mean when I say that gratitude gives me home in a small parish of love, I shall not be describing something rare of my own, or special to a happy few, but a common reality of human life. And this simple reality of our life is worth describing in our bewildered time of intellectual phantasy, institutional enslavements, and ideological nightmares.

I have learned in the years of my life that my small parish of love, where gratitude is my reality of living, is comprised chiefly of my family, my friends, and my spiritual companions. These surround me, as the days and the years move on, with a changing parish of persons. There come the days of sorrow and suffering when one of them dies or another of them turns away in coldness, or the day of blight when I myself turn as it were dead toward one of them; and there come the days of rejoicing when my family is enlarged by a child or the marriage of a child or the coming of a grandchild, or new brothers or sisters or nephews or nieces, and the adding of cousins, and the lovely days when some stranger new met becomes a friend, and the sudden days when I encounter a new spiritual companion among the sons of men, as it was on the day of delight in my youth when I first, in one of his books, encountered the to me companionable spirit of Joseph Conrad, or as it was on a day nearly forty years later when I first entered into spiritual companionship with Martin Buber in response to the the work of his life.

Of my family and my friends I speak my gratitude in brief and general terms, for the analogy between my human life and other human lives is so plain.

I was born and nurtured of a father and mother, as they were before me, in the great chain of being and the good warmth of human bondage; I had the good fortune to have brothers and a sister, to have uncles and aunts and cousins; the goodness of marriage came to me, and the goodness of children and grandchildren, and the goodness of nieces and nephews. This family in which my life has meaning, and for which I am grateful, is not an institution; it is a living reality, and my life is real in the midst of it. It is not a thing of idea; it is a reality of human communion. These are living people, bound to me by close ties of human bondage, and I am one of them, bound to them by close ties of human bondage: and among us gratitude is a foundation of a tender and responsible communion. The intensities and intimacies of love may vary; but gratitude is the foundation of this communion.

My friends are like the friends in the lives of any other man or woman or child. Once they were strangers; now they are friends. In our world of gad-about from here to there, I am like so many —a move of place of living a thousand miles away slackens some bonds of old friendships and weaves new ones in new places; but gratitude remains the ground of friendship. And friendship, like family, is not an institution—it is not a church or a state or a corporation—but a living and changing reality, a continual deep meaning of new being.

I am sure that in the emerging aeons of human life these two, family and friends, were the beginning of the parish of love in which we dwell. Our spiritual companions are companions who come later, with the emergence and development of the word. By the word I mean any form of remembered or recorded communication. By a remembered word in the family I may become the spiritual companion of a great-grandfather I never saw. By recorded word—a primitive painting on a cave in Spain, a Bible of a people, a sonata of Mozart, or a lyric of Keats—I may be given spiritual companionship in the lives of others whom I do not meet in immediate flesh.

Just as I am grateful at large for being a son of the people of earth, so I am grateful at large for being an inheritor of the spiritual giving of their lives of a multitude of toilers of spirit who have informed their fellow men of the useful, the sacred, the beautiful, and the good. This is the Great Parish of Man and God. A whole life long could not tell its multitudinous beads of gratitude.

But I speak of a few spiritual companions in my own small parish of love who have helped me live, by these few representing many more. I speak of them somewhat in the time order in which their companionship came to me in my need and comforted and helped me. And I say of them, as of family and friends, that these companions are not an institution but living reality of the life I have been given and have tried in reality to live.

The first and last companion of my spirit is God.

I know this is the most terrible thing a man can say, and the one which if wrongly said will surely destroy me. But I have to say it, for it is; and if I say it wrong, I am destroyed. Then I have to say it, for if I do not say it, I have had no family, no friends, and no companions, and would lie to say I had. That God has been my spiritual companion has been the deepest wound of all my life, for I have failed Him. That God has been my spiritual companion has been the deepest gratitude of all my life, and in my deepest failure and sharpest wound, my heart has still turned in trust toward Him. I shall not say that I was ever man enough to love God, in simple love of full communion, but only that all my life has been a longing and a trying so to love God as to break the heart of agony and restore the heart of peace. I could not begin in gratitude if I said less; I might enter destruction if I tried to say more.

All the other companions of spirit who have helped me live have been those whose lives and work have helped me live in gratitude toward earth and creature and toward man and God. One of them said ages ago—and I sometimes pause on the corner of Fifth Avenue and 65th Street at Temple Emmanuel in New York to see his words carved there in stone: "Do justly. Love mercy. And walk humbly with thy God."

The voices of the Bible have companioned my life, and I know not how I would have been able to live unless Ruth and David and Job and Micah and Isaiah had spoken to me, and Jesus had spoken to me. I am what is called "of an American Protestant family"; but that is not the heart of the matter. The heart of the matter is that I am of God; the great voices of the Bible, offering spiritual companionship to me, have spoken to me of God. It is very real to me, very reality of my life, that Micah stands me still on Fifth Avenue in New York and speaks to me, that I have sat and read and heard the words and touched companionship with Jesus on a dry old log beside wildflowers in a mountain forest, that the sweet trust and love of Ruth has spoken to me on the sway of a ship on the ways of ocean, and that the song of David has comforted my heart in deep tunnels of a coal mine. It is very real to me that great voices of the Bible have been here and now with me in the days of my life.

And others, of other great religions of man, have given me kindly light. Light of spiritual companionship has come into my life and helped me, not from institutions, but from children of light and of God.

And so it was not the state or the union or man as a political animal that comforted me with spiritual companionship with Lincoln when I was a boy. I was sometimes a deeply troubled boy. Here, by his life and word and work revealed, was a man among men, deeply alive in the throes of time and the troubles of place. And of deepest suffering he said, "This, too, will pass away"; and in simple compassion he said: "With malice toward none, with charity toward all. . . ."

Surely by now it becomes clear the sort of spiritual companionship I mean for which I am lifelong grateful. I need try to make no case, but only name a few more to represent many.

Emerson stirred my heart with delightful daring and vault of spirit, and I think no year of my life passes that I do not turn to him for company in spiritual hazard.

It came upon me as a boy that, like a certain whorl in the print of my thumb, there was set in me somewhat of a gift of words, and I was bewildered and timid that in our athletic and practical society I should have so odd a gift. It seemed like a lonely and sissy thing to sit in a room and try, by reality of memory and by imagination also serving reality, to say in words some song of my heart. At this time I first read a book by Conrad—and met, not a book, but a man. It was worthy of a man to do what I as a boy was trying to learn to do. And Conrad became my companion in long long labors of memory and imagination serving reality to bring forth word of song.

Others came into this world of poetry where so much of the work of my life has been done: Cervantes with those two marvelous fellows of my spirit, Don Quixote and Sancho Panza. Shakespeare, with his singing of man, so wide and deep, became a voice, a wisdom, a courage, and an astonishment of song to me. Montaigne told me a thousand things about myself and our common life, and now that I am more nearly his age, I see their deepening truth. Rembrandt is not a painter of pictures but a man I see face to face in his work, and both in moments of suffering and moments of mystery I have sat before one of his pictures and been companioned by his spirit in my need. I have done this in New York, in Washington, in Amsterdam, and in Paris. I have spoken of Beethoven at Tanglewood; and I have sat with Aeschylus on the brow of Cadillac Mountain on the coast of Maine, returning to the spirit of his words on a mountain by the sea, and I have needed his tragic restraint to teach me to cast not the seed of reckless words and crop the land with woe. There was a time when my chief guide among the philosophers was Santayana, lovely in the language of nostalgic soliloquy, a very lonely companion, really, who never openly told his love of God. Thomas More told and laughed and lived his love of God, and for it died: "I am the King's good servant, but God's first." I once spent months writing a play based on the life of Thomas More; it is one of the best things I ever wrote, and well it might be, for about two-thirds of all there is in it are his own words. And companionship with him and with his family and his good friends, learned Erasmus, courageous Warham, and Colet so deeply sweet of heart, was a lifting up of my life by great good men. And I would not know half so well what meeting a man or a woman or a child may be, had not the deep spirit of Martin Buber come to companion my life in these my later years when I am trying to make gift of good deep human song of love and of gratitude.

So it is as I have told, and yet profoundly more than I have told, that gratitude, reality, and meaning of my life are deeply founded in a small parish of love, my family and my friends and companions of my spirit; and in this here and now of my life, gratitude is my home in the presence of God.

And sometimes, as we venture further, into the Great Parish of Man and God, divine occasions of gratitude set deep light alight in our lives, as it was with me when I was blessed by the Sleepers Of Oaxaca, or when first I saw that living act of gratitude in stone and glass, the Cathedral of Chartres, or first breathed in the dim great and musical spaces of the Cathedral in Seville, or as it was with Keats upon first looking into Chapman's Homer:

> "Then felt I like some watcher of the skies
>   When a new planet swims into his ken;
> Or like stout Cortez when with eagle eyes
>   He star'd at the Pacific—and all his men
> Look'd at each other with a wild surmise—
>   Silent, upon a peak in Darien."

Here and now, in the parish of our heart, small or great, gratitude is our home and our blessing and our wild surmise in the presence of God's giving of continual new creation.

For here is of God's infinity, and now is of God's eternity: Man is born, man lives, and man dies—I and Thou are born and live and die—in no lesser time and no lesser place.

And by our gratitude here and now we hallow our life to one another and to God.

2 & *Our Life in One Another*

Theme and Variations

A revelation comes to us, and it is beautiful in giving and promise of life. It is a sacred event, an occasion of God, a moment that touches us to be holy. It is a profound mystery that illuminates our unknowing with a music and a wave of immortal light. It came to Israel at Sinai, it came to Job out of the whirlwind, it came to Paul on the road to Damascus and to Buddha under the great tree. It is a great command:

"Thou shalt be holy!"

And the astonishing mystery that illuminates our unknowing and our unbelief is the implication in it that we may be holy, that divinity so deeply touches us and so searchingly illuminates our frail mortality that we may respond by being holy. This is our dialogue with God, and our human words are too little an answer.

"Thou shalt be holy."

"Thou hast made me. I face Thee."

Even this may be too many words.

To be there in utter rendering of our life toward God is our wordless answer.

But we are prone to freeze the Mystery in words, and of words make a stumbling block to life. We would put into words what the revelation is and set forth a doctrine of how to fulfill it. Instead of rendering life to the revelation, we would worship a Platonic Idea, an Aristotelian Category, an Analysis by Paul, an Edict of Augustine, a Proof by Aquinas or Maimonides, a Dialectic of Hegel or Marx, a Psychologism by Freud or Jung. And a drive for finite exactness breaks the heart in loss of living mystery. A truly profound melancholy comes upon us in our failure to fulfill the letter and law of Mystery that has been frozen into words. It is the most profound spiritual anguish in the depths of our religious life, and if we haven't been sharply tormented by it ourselves, we certainly know of it from the suffering among saints. But we do know of it ourselves. It is said that we shall be holy, and we know that we are not.

Yet we may be toward holiness, and torment ourselves because we are not, according to this freeze of words or that freeze of words, perfectly holy; we may, like Luther, therefore consider ourselves unworthy to be, or, like Nietzsche, consider therefore that

God is dead, or, like Simone Weil, seek extreme absolution of absolute suffering.

I cannot fetch down God to the measure of my words, nor mete out a formula of how to answer Him, but can only try to live the dialogue Mystery offers to me.

For our immeasurable dialogue with God there are no sufficient words. But for the humble dialogue between man and man— between I and Thou—there may be words of comfort. A man may try to confirm and to comfort those he loves by searching the gratitude of his heart and speaking what he finds. I shall try.

To be a Single One, dreaming there is only myself and God, or only myself as God, is root of horror indeed; but also let us not dream that I and Thou can enter into any reality, build any spiritual home, by breaking the great, deep, and enriching bonds of human bondage and setting ourselves up as the only two of God, as ourselves Twin God. To be a Single One is a dream of pride; to be a Twin God is a dream of passion; and both dreams shall wither our hearts in an ultimate horror.

Do you know the sweet gratitude of divine awakening into the continual new creation of our immortal human bondage? Perhaps to be one of all the billions on earth and whoever lived and whoever shall come hereafter is too great for the immediate gratitude of our humble hearts; none short of Jesus was ever so fully a man, so utterly a son of God. But I know and Thou knowest the small sweet gratitude of dwelling not alone in our own small parish of love.

But even here, at humble center of our living, not one of our relations to any other is perfect. I have been troubled to understand this thing, so dear and lovely at the heart of my life, to understand it so that I may sing my gratitude for it and be understood by thee, my friend, and thee, my friend, and thou stranger coming near to be my friend. Is it possible to love, but not love perfectly? For me to love another is theoretically an absolute; must it then be true that because I love many I love none? And what

if one who loves me loves another? Is that perfidy? And what if
our love for one differs from our love for another? Is it therefore
not love?

Martin Buber's book of gratitude and joy and song of relation,
I and Thou, has deepened my understanding of these things; but
already others, not Buber, are beginning to call it "a philosophy,"
are beginning to freeze its mystery and song into rational absolutes,
and even the reader himself—I reading, you reading—begins to
read into this lovely song rules, strictures, and preventive absolutes.
This troubles my heart, and I seek comfort, not in the Mystery of
Perfection, but in the more humble mystery of my own frailty. I
know I have no perfect giving of my life in relation, but I do
know I have relation; I know I love imperfectly, but I love.

We do become persons and real, and our life becomes real, in
our meeting with one another. That which I shall here call grace—
and it could be called joy—takes place not in either one of us, I or
Thou, but between the two of us within the watch of God. It is
toward perfection.

Our human mind leaps to absolutes; we would bind a flower in
a genus, a man in a species, and God in the chains of a category.
We will write and impose upon ourselves (or do it in thought and
speaking) our Summa Flora, our Summa Philosophia, our Summa
Theologica. And so it is with I and Thou. We make it categorical.
There is an I and Thou relationship conceivable to us in perfect
form; that is, a perfect meeting between two persons, in each of
whom trust and unreserve toward the other is unconditional, their
mutuality being infinite, and the presence of God between them
absolute. This is an ideal concept of an utterly fulfilled meeting in
total reality. Perhaps it can and does happen to two of us in an
instant of spontaneity. There is a sense in which it cannot happen
less than perfectly; that is the sense of our potential perfect being.
But this perfect touch of God between us, this Absolute Grace,
except for the perfect potential of the spontaneous instant—the
moment of eternity—has duration in our mortal time and im-

perfection. It is an immortal rune of God brought to song in a mortal heart; and our stings of clay imperfectly resound the chords of God. For our reins are formed of dust, as the Bible says it, or, as moderns say, we are formed of a few things like carbon, phosphorous and iron mixed in a lot of water, which is a sort of mud. Without divinity we are mud; but we are not able to be always or entirely divine.

So it is that I think of what I call my small parish of love, that presence in my life of a number of people I love and whose love I accept. They are welcome indwellers in my heart, and I want to be a welcome indweller in each of their hearts. There has been between us, between myself and each one of them, a beginning in a meeting in—at least perhaps—a perfect instant of spontaneity. But in the duration thereafter of the touch of God between us there is great variety of imperfection.

I am, I think in common with many sons and daughters of man, more profoundly subject to absolutes of cumulative human thought than I am inclined to realize. We are imbued with thoughtless obedience to authority of thought. Three powerful sources of this (and there are others) have been theology, law, and science. Thinking in these realms—and they blanket our remembrance and our prudence, and hush the call of reality—aims at absolutes. So and so is once for all; and thou shalt not listen to the Still Small Voice! Far more than we realize, we again and again conclude that if a thing is not *just so,* it is nothing. If faith is not exactly according to dogma, it is not faith; if a contract is not exactly according to law, it is not a contract; if the behavior of material is not according to the laws science has set down for this, it is not the behavior of material.

I and Thou get to thinking that if an I-Thou relationship is not according to the perfection of the ideal instant of spontaneity, then it is not a meeting and not a relationship. Instead of being grateful that we are simple persons of human bondage on earth, we loathe ourselves for not being infinite gods in the sky. We love; sufficient unto the day we love; and we do not know it, because it is so humble; and in our strange delusion that we must have it All Or Nothing, we turn aside from the true little we are, we analyze, scold and hate, and mutter misery that I am zero in the sun and thou art zero in the sun. And sometimes it is our plain cowardice, running from responsibility: because I cannot give thee all I am in unreserve, I give thee of myself nothing at all.

I remember when I was a boy one of my brothers and I rented a field for a summer outside of Omaha; and we went out there on our bicycles and we planted and cultivated and harvested a crop of potatoes. We did not buy perfect seed-potatoes; we did not perfectly plow, fertilize, and seed that field; we did not perfectly keep the rows clean of weeds; we did not dig up our potatoes at the perfect moment of perfectly fulfilled growth, and as we grubbed them out, we did not get them all. But they were potatoes; my brother and I husbanded their growing; and they did feed people. A thousand farmers in Nebraska that summer raised better crops and bigger crops of potatoes; but my brother and I raised and harvested sixty bushels of potatoes, and they were food of life to men and women and children. Of many sizes, they were all potatoes. We rejoiced together: each one of them was a potato!

I know, in my small parish of love, of many varieties and degrees of relationship—as real as potatoes; of repeated meeting and continued relationship, of communication in depths nearly perfect and communication only fitfully and tenuously warmed by, as it were, a further away sun of perfection. And I know that each of these relationships with those I love and whose love I accept or would accept if they chose to offer it, and who are welcome in my heart any time they offer their presence and any time my remembrance or prayer renders them present to me—each of these relationships is real, each was mutually generated in the beginning meeting, each contains an undying degree, however small, of mutuality, and every one of them always faces, from however far off, toward the potential perfection of perfect beginning and perfect recurrence of meeting. Gratitude opens my heart, and I know this. It simply is not true to our imperfect human living to hold that an I-Thou relationship must be fulfilled in its perfect form or it is not communion at all. Neither is it real, in fear that we must be perfect or nothing, to pretend that the imperfection of our relation with one another is perfect.

There are other troubles too, besides this one of imperfection, that bewilder us with doubt of the meaning and reality of our relation with one another. If we are caught in the grasp of the concept of meaninglessness—the intellectual illusion that life is absurd, that there are no true values, that we are but a tattered dream fabricated by our own psyche, and so on—then we mistake variety of manifestation to be a negation of reality. And yet we do live a variety of manifestations of relation, and real essence of relation is in them. Each one is a real potato, however odd its shape or size.

We may distress ourselves that we have failed to meet one another and failed in dialogue of life together because we remember a sublime and torrential first sweep of meeting, and that has not remained continuous. Must we be forever Niagara Falls? Sublime force of mutual relation between us in great flow of unreserve is not continuous. The Niagara River has its shallows and quiet pools, its somewhere beginning and its somewhere onflowing, as well as its falls, and in each moment of its way it is a river.

A flower of grace blooms between us. The throes of life and the hazards of mortality sweep us into the regions of grief or press us down the steeps of pain; there are winters of the heart and a death of flowers, there are dark nights of soul and a folding and sleeping of flowers; and at other times we yield ourselves to the coldness of ambition, lust, power, position, and frost the petals of grace. But when gratitude returns warmth to the root of life, the flower of grace blooms again.

We are bewildered, too, by the many forms in which our dialogue in our own small parish of love may be real and good. Some would like it to be always and only kissing. But we speak to one another in word, in act, in gesture and glance, together in stillness or together in dance; though far apart we touch one another in a letter through the mail, in the gift of a sea shell left on

the doorstep, and also in thought. There is a spiritual companionship that is not illusion. There is a dialogue of being present to
one another that is very real, and not to be mistaken for the monologue of self-generated phantasy. An absent companion becomes
present to me when reality of memory and reality of imagination
open my heart to his presence. Perhaps, as a man who has written
many books, I have a vivid sense of this reality of spiritual companionship. In lifelong work such as this, one learns what is
speaking in true communion and what is forlorn illusion in monologue or perhaps merely fantastical. I could not have written
in any reality of Saint Ambrose, unless first I had met reality of his
spirit in the records of history and the sayings of his life in his own
writings; nor of Thomas More; I could not have written a remembrance of my friendship with Thomas Wolfe in any reality, without
strict reality of memory of our friendship and without holding my
imagination strictly to his reality, and not free to my own mono-
logical meandering. Even fictional characters I have "invented"
have reality in so far as my sense of their being is traceable to real
persons in real life. When I say I have relation and companionship
with a person present to my thought, I mean that person is other
than myself and real to me in thought, remembrance, and prayer,
is real and other than myself. I am not totally lost to my wife and
my children and my friends when miles and days separate us, but
in spiritual companionship do live one of the realities of relation
between us. This present work of thanksgiving to many and to God
has an almost total reality of memory and a very real service of
imagination to reality underlying every passage in it. I have not
invented my life or my gratitude or my small parish of love or God.
I also know the monologue of self-with-self, the daydreaming illusion of relation that is not relation, the conversation of ghosts
within, and the outward action that treats another not as a person
but as a tool or a convenience or a nuisance, and these are things
of escape or illness, of arrogance or coldness; they are breaks and
losses in life, from which by gratitude we may be returned to life.

From the knowing of gratitude in my own life, I take many an

I-Thou meeting between two of us, and offer a series of interpreta-
tions of how the original touch of God between us may have subse-
quent duration in our human dialogue in real and various forms
and intensities. For reality of my living experience of I-Thou
relations in my own small parish of love has revealed to me that
the intellectual realm of ideas, which calls for the absolute-thing-in-
itself or nothing, is transcended by the intelligible realm of poetry,
in which we in our meetings form, in mutual generation, real
poems of human imperfect relation; and that God transcends man
in every realm of man, so that more things are possible, more
things do happen, more things are real than we by our minds
can apprehend. And often each one of us more deeply and richly
lives in many I-Thou relationships, and in each I-Thou relationship, than we acknowledge in our conscious thought or in our
statements to one another, for neither our thought nor our language can fully encompass the abundant reality of being. There
are no doubt more possible varieties of real mutual relationship
than I suggest in the list to come; but I name as many as I do,
because I have often been puzzled or even troubled in my relation
with another person, when either one of us, or both of us, was
confused as to the reality of our communion, confused by its reality,
its degree, its nature, and its continual variability. (A grandchild
sat on my wife's lap, and the relation was visibly real; the same
grandchild sent her a drawing of delight from three thousand miles
away, and the relation, invisible, was real.)

The following tabulation helps open my heart and mind in gratitude to the multiple wonder, goodness, and new creation possible
to each I-Thou occasion of God.

I and Thou are met in real meeting, and the grace of life, the
touch of God, is real between us. This reality is the ground of vari-
ation:

I. Each of us is blessed by the living grace between us, and each
of us has participated with grace in blessing the life of the other;
and this touch of God enriches every other love of each one of us.

II. No such meeting is like any other such meeting, whether it be another meeting between I and Thou, or meetings between either one of us and other thous. Each meeting is unique in its quality and in its degree of perfection, and no meeting, however faintly perfect, is without divine grace of a touch of God. Each instant, each form of communication—communion—between two persons, I and Thou, is real, mutual, and holy.

III. Both I and Thou may acknowledge the blessing of the meeting, and then go about our separate ways never to touch one another in communion again. This is a root with one divine flower.

IV. Either I or Thou, or both of us, may deny that the original blessing was real. This is the lie against existence, and withers many flowers in the life that utters it. If only one of us two denies the original blessing, the other who acknowledges it is as if he had given his life to God in hostage for the one who denies it, and this may bring a turning of the other toward life again. And he who offers his life in meeting to another, whether or not that other knows or accepts or responds, has rendered his life to God and is deeply enriched by the reality and gratitude of giving. For though our speaking of our life to another may not be heard or answered by that one, it is heard and answered by God, and our speaking to anyone who hears has become deeper song.

V. Both I and Thou, in gratitude toward the original blessing, by continued spiritual work in mutual communication and trust, may achieve lifelong friendship from this original blessing, which is a bush of a thousand flowers, and each of them is a radiant blossom. It is perhaps most often and most beautifully grown between us in marriage.

VI. Because of our mortality, either or both of us may die before the original blessing flowers in further fulfillment. If only one of us dies, the other may nourish the divine flower in remembrance.

VII. One of the two of us may labor to raise from the root of the original blessing the radiant bush of enduring friendship and a thousand blossoms, while the other, though acknowledging the original blessing, turns entirely away from further communion.

VIII. The life of either one who labors for many blossoms (or of both, if both labor) is enriched, even though there is failure in communication; for where intention of our heart is toward nourishing the touch of God, we are more deeply enabled to live in all our other loves, even though this one fails to respond.

IX. One of the two of us may labor with a large unreserve for the radiant bush, and the other, with a far more reserved mutuality, may resist so rich a flowering (for how often can any one of us complete all of our loves in each of our loves?) but resist in real presence of person, now by silence, now by disagreement, now by retreat, now by dialogue of thanks, but always still holding communication sacred; and thus a mutual generation of new being continues between I and Thou; and, though the radiant bush of a thousand flowers does not flourish, a modest plant of real mutual life grows and bears new lovely blossoms; and all our loves—each love of thine, each love of mine—are nourished by this beauty. Because it is rare for any one of us to be utterly open to each one he meets, but each of us is normally more open toward one, less toward another, more now, less another time, more again, yet never utterly closed against the touch of God, this is probably our most common form of hallowed I-Thou relation. Each of us, in our own small parish of love, must know of real and hallowed relations of unequal mutuality; now one, now the other, is the more unreservedly responsive, the more able to give and to receive; but our faintest opening of our heart to mutuality lets in the touch of God.

X. Both of us may acknowledge the original blessing of meeting and binding one to another in communion, then repose in passive readiness to receive grace of new meeting, if new meeting should befall us, leaving it to accidents of social motion in time and space whether or not this should be, but not rising in search of one another. The abundance of God sometimes blesses again even this passiveness of ours.

I could think of other possible variations in this central beauty and holiness of our human communion with one another, and of them all the only one that deserves the name of evil is the lie against existence; every other one is mutual giving of life and receiving of life between us, and is holy. Each of us has no human home alone; and though it may be true that, in some rare instances (I have never known of one, and to imagine it is like trying to imagine infinity) one of us may find entire home in a single other heart and give entire home to that heart, most of us in ordinary life need home in more hearts than one. And every homecoming and every welcoming home is sacred and hallows this life between us.

Our heart is stayed in human warmth, and is comforted, by each of our loves for each one we love, and by each love of each one who loves us; and each of our loves is nearness to God.

3 🙣🙡 *Gratitude Keeps No Books*

A Meditation

I have learned by my long life in my own small parish of love this delightful wonder:

Gratitude keeps no books.

A grateful heart keeps no books, and has no need of a clerk in the heart to keep track of the sweet influences of life, of giving and receiving of life between us. There is no certified public accountant in my parish keeping book on grace and beauty. Institutions keep balance in policy and power, rule in and rule out members; business keeps tracks of accounts receivable and accounts payable; law keeps track of *quid pro quo;* politics keeps running balance of favors and counts the rolling of logs; and even in our social life some of us think in terms of due bills: a letter for a letter, an invitation for an invitation, a party for a party. But in our true parish of love we keep no books.

What a mean and meager life it would be to keep books on love and friendship, to keep books on the presence of God!

I gave Susie a kiss and a hug; she gave me only a hug; she owes me a kiss.

I sewed twenty stitches in my darling's jacket; he owes a corner of the moon.

Helped Joe roof his barn; he owes me day in hayfield.

Given to God: Received from God:

37½ seconds of prayer   Not a wink

Double entry bookkeeping, indeed!

When my heart is grateful, gratitude frees me to give, to offer, to sing. I do not have to keep accounts on whether anyone or anyone else makes return. Gratitude sends out no due bills to anyone for anything, for it is free to give. It is free to give once or twice or endlessly again. And in gratitude I do not have to wait for someone else to give or love or trust. I can begin.

Job presented God with a due bill—so much righteousness for so much favor expected—until the Voice out of the whirlwind taught him dialogue with God, and bookkeeping between Job and God was done with.

The gratitude of dialogue between two of us puts an end to the folly of keeping book on love, on trust, on giving all gift of life we are able to give.

4 ❧ *Our Parish in the City of God*

A Thanksgiving

The City of God is never closed to a grateful heart; and our own small parish of love is a part of the City of God, which our own gratitude holds open to others, and we welcome one another in out of the wasteland in joy together.

It is a far cry, and a disastrous one, from *The City Of God* of Augustine in the fourth century to the *Wasteland* of Eliot in the twentieth century, when it is a common opinion that an up-to-date mind should give no credence to the reality of God, saying with

Nietzsche that He is dead, or, with Freud, Jung and Fromm, that He is but a metaphor left over from psychic immaturity. Augustine, in an age of spiritual collapse, toiled his way through Greek humanism, Roman pragmatism and Manichean dualism toward the City of God. It was not a metaphor, but his life. And Eliot's wasteland is not a metaphor, but a modern life desolate in anguish and dreary in our day of resentment, anger and slaughter. But a modern human being, as well as a Roman, may toil and turn away from the stews and frets of spiritual collapse toward the sanity of trust in life, toward tender and responsible communion with another human being, toward companionship with God. This will not be a metaphor, but your life and my life really lived. The melancholia that blasts our age is not an inevitable fate.

Our true word is not spoken alone, our true work is not done alone, our true venture is not dared alone, our true love is not flowered alone, our true becoming is not fulfilled alone; in each hallowed moment of our true reality many others and God are with us, and enable us, and we are immeasurably not alone.

And when I and Thou are met, we are present to one another in new creation of ineffable reality. We are with God.

And gratitude is our home in the City of God.

5 🙖 *Tender Song of Man and Woman*

Two Songs of Life

My heart is moved to tender human song of all my life, the sudden song of a man to the woman of all his life, rejoicing in gratitude in the grace of God between us. How lovely have been our deepening years, child of heart and child of heart, met in this world of God! I and Thou in all trust of trying, in unreserve of forgiving and love, living unto one another, and in trust toward those we love, in this world of God!

I

Begin with music out of earth,
  Through slumber ringing;
My darling comes in fertile mirth,
  Her laughter bringing.

She Sings
  First my nimble fingers,
  Then my parting lips,
Last my merry, sudden eyes
  Escape tenfold caresses.

He Sings
You have wanton charms
  To delay me,
But no fateful harms
  To dismay me.

First I brush your fingers,
  Now I seal your lips,
Last I close your sudden eyes
  With ten amazéd kisses.

She Sings
I have wanton charms
  To delay you,
But no fateful harms
  To dismay you.

He Sings
  First I bind your shoulders,
  Then I bind your waist,
Last I bind your wanton heart
  In tenfold embrace.

She Sings

My wild love,
My warm love,
My fertile love is taken.

He Sings

Your warm heart,
Your wild heart
Shall never be forsaken.

End with music out of earth,
    Through slumber sounding;
My darling came in fertile mirth,
    With love abounding.

II

Thou and I,
Beloved!

Our time is given to us,
In this world of God
Corruptible by man,
In time of sweeps of anger,
In time of blacks of slaughter,
When the unleashed passions of man
Seed misery and disaster,
Spread storms of human chaos,
In all the places of people,
In all the hearts of people;
There is poise of terror,
There is shatter of horror,
And there is sound of fury
All about us,
And echoed in us;
And we stand in human bondage,
Touched of God to one another.

I and Thou
Beloved!

We dwell beside our fire,
Which is Light between us,
In day's end peace,
And peace of many years,
Immeasurably not alone
In peace of many years;
And we are here in grace
Of human bondage
Unto one another,
Deep in our living years,
Unto one another.

How have been the years unto thee
And unto me
In our life between us?

I range remembrance,
And take deep sounding
Of here and now,
Gathering rays of light
Which I shall shine as glad as morning
Upon your face and mine
In song
Of Thou and I living.

For you have made our home
A place of light
And a place of song,
And my song and my heart
Have been beside you;
And our hands have touched
Our children
And our grandchildren

In peace and in love,
And touched friends and strangers
In peace and in love.

We have danced in starlight,
And rejoiced in the morning,
And worked in the day,
And wept, and each of us has wept;
And we have had much mercy
Unto one another,
And tried and toiled and loved and lived,
Until a depth of becoming
Beautiful to one another,
Entrusted each to the other,
Is our humble glory of human song;
And our grateful love abides
The root and crown of our tree of life
In the Light of God.

Thou and I
Beloved!

We stand in human bondage,
Touched of God to one another,
In corruptible time
Of man-made horror;
And where two stand met with God,
And abide with God,
In present storm of human chaos,
Amid terror of people,
Amid sorrow of people,
Horror shall not prevail,
But life shall spread,
And light shall spread,
And song shall spread.

Thou and I are song of God,
Beloved,
Joined to song of others,
And Song shall spread.

And joy abides in the song of a man to the woman of his life, rejoicing in gratitude in deepening years unto one another in this world of God.

6 🐦🐦 *Gratitude in the Realm of Love*

An Essay

Do you know the forming power of gratitude in all the realms of love? Do you know the healing miracle of gratitude in all the wounds of love? Do you know the restoring grace of gratitude in all the dyings of love?

We are in profoundest need of gratitude to begin our love, to nourish our love, and to save our love.

In the lived beatitude of a human life, that most to be grateful for is that we love; and gratitude liberates us to love, to offer and to accept love. Our human love is subject to imbalance and dissonance among the drives of passion—dread, hate, jealousy, greed, lust, pride; and gratitude has great power to hold love in sweet balance and tender harmony. Such obsessional madness as poets find in Eros (the *amo et odi* of Catullus, the ambivalent love-hate of Freud); the ideological insanity that today corrupts Philia (as in political murder and war); and the religious righteousness that poisons Agape (as in denying truth to be in others, in excommunications and burnings at the stake)—none of these cruel corruptions of the heart of man is let loose to destroy in a love that is nourished by gratitude.

In all the realms of our human love, unless there be gratitude, the fierce intensities of passion seize upon us and make a torment of wounded and unbalanced love.

All my love begins in gratitude. When I feel sweet, good, balanced, harmonious, and warm in my heart toward another, and a smile of knowing and affirming the reality and goodness of another illuminates my being, then I am grateful. It is the sun rising up in the day of my life. Although it seems to me that gratitude is sometimes touched awake in me by grace, and sometimes wakened in me by the coming near of another, and sometimes found by prayer and courage, still I do not know how I become grateful, how this sun rises up in the day of my life; in my unknowing, gratitude is God's declaration of life. But when I do become grateful, this gratitude is ground for fresh responsive living; it liberates my heart to give forth affection, frees me to choose to love, to return to love, to abide in love, and to offer to each one I love my whole and illumined word, illumined touch, and illumined deed.

Only in gratitude am I utterly free to give my life.

The word I say of love to another is inaudible until the other's reply of love makes real the song of life between us. The word I say of love shall haunt the air inaudible, until response in love makes music of the song of life in air and light between I and Thou.

And by our gratitude we shall sing and lift our lives up to radiance, helping one another.

7 ❧ To Each One I Love

A Song of Life

I sang a song of my life in the morning.

I rose before dawn of a Christmas day, in this house where I live, while my wife was asleep and my children were asleep and my grandchildren were asleep, and I made a song to each one I love. When they awakened, I gave it to them, and gave it later to my friends, and put it in the local paper for the people of the town where I live. And now I sing it here, in word of life, where it may sing and wait and listen for fulfillment of our human song:

> Thou art my friend, and I shall hold thee dear
> In gentle ways that beat dread darkness down;
> I met thee in the peace of "God is here!"
> And shall not hide from God what is His own.
> I know our day of darkened soul distraught,
> Cloyed full of easements down into despair,
> In evil swirl of violence overtaught,
> And sleazy horror haunting everywhere.
> It is my simple thing to lift my face
> So thou shalt know that thou hast met a friend
> Within God's watch of living peace and grace:—
> When two have met with God is horror's end.
>   Look for God's legend always in my eye:
>   Abide in my heart at peace until I die.

8 These Are My Loves

An Apostrophe

And these are my loves that I shall name and tell:

Thou art my beloved with whom I dwell in deepening light of gratitude fulfilling all our years and enriching all our loves, known to one another in laughter and embrace, to one another known in our suffering and our joy and our peace; and we live in song, responding to one another in the daily return of the ceaseless occasions of God.

Thou art my child, and I love and shelter thee. In the years of growing thou art also soon to be my friend, with sheltering of one another become equal between us. And gratitude makes holy our tenderness to one another in the touch of God between us.

Thou art my friend, thou man, thou woman, thou child; thou

art by brother, my sister, my neighbor, my friend, and thou art the stranger new met and loved. We meet in gratitude and take sweet counsel together. We are a light to one another, glowing in the greater light of God, and our love stands established in gratitude, and we give home to one another.

Thou art my God, I love Thee. I love Thee in gratitude as Thy lifted up and living mortal child, touched by Thee to life amid all there is that Thou hast given form and being; and gratitude opens my heart to bless Thee. For Thou art my God in all my knowing; and beyond all my knowing, Thou art my God.

9 ❧ *In Name and Praise of Gratitude*
A Word of Trust in Life

Do you know the harmonizing light of gratitude in all the realms of love? How it forms our love? How it heals our love? How it saves our love?

Our gratitude is warmth of life given to warmth of life, and in warmth of life returned.

In name and praise of gratitude, Thou and I shall meet with God and live.

Book Six

Gratitude
and Suffering

1 🙚 *Gratitude and Suffering*

A Mystery

How shall I sing in praise of gratitude in our world so full of pain? I am a man. I know the heart of agony. I have wept. I stand delivered into the dust of death, and still I sing. I know the pain of being a man, until a thousand weary pains foregather in the entire suffering of the one deepest wound of all my life, until I cannot cry out: "My God, my God, why hast Thou forsaken me?" but can only weep in wordless agony of heart. Delivered unto the dust of death, in our world so full of pain, how dare I sing in praise of gratitude?

I know of three things and two things that enter into this mystery of gratitude and suffering. They do not explain it, but they open my unknowing to the reality of the mystery. The three things are resentment, integrity, and mystery; and the two things are love and grief.

It may be said that a man suffers resentment, but resentment is a man's first loss of the mystery of gratitude and suffering. Resentment is a refusal of suffering, a loss of the mystery of life in anger against life. Resentment closes off my heart to trust and participation in the abundance of being, and opens my mind to imagining and executing irresponsible ferocities. Resentment is a form of death, and shuts my heart to the living mystery of suffering.

But how can a man fulfill his integrity, and not resent the illogical and unjust cruelties that crush and torment others and himself? I have learned in living that my integrity has many phases, and a final wholeness. The easiest form of integrity that tempts me to adhere to it is the integrity of my self-defense. This is both the integrity of self-survival—of doing whatever I can do not to be killed, crippled, or hurt—and the integrity of what might be called ego-maintenance—of doing whatever I can do in defense against any attack on my own spiritual comfort. In defense of this phase of our own integrity we human beings kill, cripple, and hurt others and harass or destroy their spiritual comfort in behalf of our own. It is the integrity of Narcissus adoring himself, of man for himself.

Larger than this is the integrity of Prometheus. Prometheus, in compassion for the frailty of man, the legend tells us, stole fire from the gods and gave it to man. This is the integrity of my compassion. It is offended by poverty, hunger, cold, needless disease and suffering of any kind in others. It moves us often to good and great charity of thinking and doing. We can in its name give the traveler our cloak and our friend our life. But we can also, under the guise of its name, promote resentment and violence: as, for example, a Marxian compassion for the exploited may promote programs of depersonalization, resentment, and murder.

Faustian integrity is another great phase of integrity; how shall we win and hold an absolute integrity of reason, an ultimate human fulfillment of science? Faust sold his soul to the devil to get this power the quick way. We are more patient. We study, we do research, we accumulate knowledge. We have greatly served in doing so, and have often avoided, stilled, or removed pressures of suffering by this good work. But too much worship of integrity of reason may blind us to compassion and may make us too arrogant to obey mystery. Reality is not necessarily rational. One man may hold that it is essential to his integrity as a clear thinker to deny the mystery of God. This is, indeed, a common claim of contemporary intellectual integrity. Another man may hold that compassion is not a function of the integrity of science, and thereupon proceed as if compassion were not a function of the integrity of man. All these phases of integrity—and others that could be named—become my whole integrity when, in true direction of my heart, my total person of body, mind, and spirit turns in trust and trying toward God, and suffers reality.

This is a mystery. It is not definable. It is not logical. It is not finite. It does not avoid suffering and death. It does not avoid error and failure. But it is toward survival, toward spiritual comfort, toward compassion, toward both knowledge and wisdom, toward love and toward the whole integrity of gratitude in a world full of pain.

And now I come to love and grief, wherein we so commonly and so deeply suffer.

It is easy for us to know that love is the joy of the heart; it is hard for us to learn that grief is the light of the world.

These two, in the miracle of gratitude, fulfill and bless our life.

It is easy for us to know that love is the joy of the heart that draws us unto one another in all radiance of hope; it is hard for us to learn that grief is the light of the world that lights the suffering and glory of our being unto one another in the profound illumination of compassion.

And gratitude is the miracle in the mystery of our communion in God.

And this part of my praise of gratitude—the mystery of gratitude and suffering—I shall try to tell in story and song out of my own living of it, in passages that are intimate and confiding, out of my own suffering, sorrow, compassion, and grief. If I did not have the trust to do it thus, in reality of my own suffering, it could not be a gift of trust in life to anyone else who suffers. For the mystery of gratitude and suffering is not a matter of good advice or pious platitude, but a matter of having lived it.

My whole integrity is to concede my heart in gratitude to joy and to tragedy, and to sing.

2 ❧ *Two Little Apple Trees*

A Story

Do you know two little apple trees, dancing before God among mountains? How many years their humble grace comforted my

heart, and they were my friends! Again and again, on my way from
Connecticut to Vermont to visit a man I love, I passed along the
highway near which they stood in sun or rain or snow or wind, in
a Massachusetts field with a noble view of Mount Greylock before
their dancing grace. I often stopped my automobile, at least once
or twice a year, even three times, and got out and bowed to them
my delight in their sweet and humble beauty, sometimes when
mist was on the mountains, sometimes when winter held their
limbs all bare, sometimes when they blossomed in the sun; and
their sweet and humble grace comforted my heart, and I was grateful to be within great Being with these two trees. Once I did them
simple homage for an afternoon, sitting on the ridge of a pile of
crushed stone beside the highway, while I painted a watercolor
of their bare poise and lovely dance together in earliest leafless
springtide; and something of their companion beauty graced
the water color that was my homage to them. I gave the picture as a gift of trust in life to someone who never saw the
trees.

Again this spring, after my long love of these sweet friends
dancing before God among mountains, I paused to bow them my
gratitude once more on a Sunday morning on my way to Vermont.
They were crowned with green leaves and each bore a few gay
blossoms. I saw again how truly small they were, and slight, but
nothing stiff, for they were all alive and dancing in their field;
and they were friends in my heart, of comfort, as day and day
went by. And when Friday came and I was returning home, I
slowed down as I approached their field to speak from my eye and
heart to them. Two great yellow earth-gouging machines had
broken into their field and were tearing up the earth where now
they danced in death-encroaching doom. And the great machines
gouged toward them and toward them, soon to crush them down
to earth and tear out their roots of life from the soil of God.

Roots of beauty of life were uptorn in my heart, and all along
my way home, and even at night and noon thereafter, I wept in
prophetic suffering at this murder of two trees I love.

So soon I wept. As we often do, in our unknowing of the abundance of God, I wept too soon. In my own mistrust of life I was frightened and hurt. It has so often happened to me, in my love of persons as well as of trees, that in my own mistrust of life I have been frightened and hurt too soon, that I must tell it true.

I returned that way a month later, on a lovely morning in June, and stopped my car in view of Greylock to grieve at the grave of these two friends of so many years, anxious in my suffering, and with still some rage in my heart at the murder of these trees. The bulldozers and drag-gougers had stopped gouging the earth fifty feet short of killing the two little apple trees, and the machines were gone. The trees still stand and live in the sun.

I got out of my car and stood on the road, ashamed before my living friends and God, ashamed of having mistrusted the abundance of life in advance, ashamed of having behaved a lie in the darkness of my own dread. But I was touched with forgiving gratitude that my friends still lived. Gratitude lifted me out of the bondage of shame. And I walked into the field in high grass to my knees, rejoicing in the sun of this day, more gracious and abundant than I; and I stood in the presence and shelter of each of these trees I love, and I touched each of them with my hand in gratitude.

But who shall fully disclose his gratitude for the abundance of God?

3 🐟 *The Murder of Man*

Two Songs of Sorrow

Do you know the murder of man by man, empoisoning the days of our lives? Do you remember the cruel crushing of Belgium in World War I when you were a child, and the continuance of slaughter in madness and fury at Rotterdam and Buchenwald, in Hiroshima and Hungary in the Second?

These numbered dead are nameless,
Who by our stroke of dark lie slain;
And this dark world dream,
Which slays plain men in anger,
Has laid its stain and shadow on us.

Now let us turn our faces toward them
Where they fell,
That we may know there is a light upon them,
Enkindled by their agony.

And by this light we shall see
We know these nameless dead;
Each one of them, suffering evil,
Has given up his life
For us who murdered them,
And we shall know their names, in stillness,
To be our own.

And we send our children to war. How shall we tell our sorrow
to a father and mother of a child slain in our war?

What happens to mothers whose sons are dead,—
Whose sons have bled on the fields of war,
Whose shoulders and eyes they shall see no more:
What happens to mothers whose sons are dead?

Shall we sit on the floor with their childhood blocks,
And build a city of makebelieve
Where sons won't die nor mothers grieve?
Shall we fold their clothes away in a box?

How shall we face lone, empty years,
When never their sturdy steps draw near,
With never their shoulders nor eyes for cheer,
Till memory dies and there are no tears?

What happens to mothers whose sons are dead?

4 🌿 *To Know Agony*

A Confession

How shall I sing in praise of gratitude in a world we so fill with pain?

Real knowing of the broken heart of our agony turns me more profoundly in tender surrender of gratitude toward each one I love. For I am old enough now to understand that the deepest wound of my life, which has smitten and shattered me, shall never be healed, unless by God. Each of us has such a wound, no two the same, that only God can heal, for no one less than God can entirely accept our imperfection, the murder we do and the love we fail, and our failure to live as fully one of God as He made us. Suffering is our maze of agony and gratitude our encounter with God. I, too, have been lost in the maze of our agony, and have lost the turn to God, and have stood delivered unto the dust of death in the deepest wound of my life.

Our suffering of love is profound and sane. Our selfish suffering is our approach to madness. So long as I can suffer and love I am sane. It is when I begin to hate that I begin to go mad. When I hate my enemy I begin to go mad; when I hate my God, I have gone mad. And sometimes, in my miserable madness, I seek suffering in hatred of myself.

I can sing no song in pity of myself for selfish suffering, for then I am mad and know not how to sing. Self in rage of self knows only how to curse.

But out of the suffering of love my heart has borne many and often a song.

5 ❧ *The Wound of Reality*

Songs of Compassion

We suffer reality in our love and our living sometimes as an exalted and uplifting joy, in a radiance and exaltation almost too divine for our mortality. I know I have been shaken out of torpid drowse and routine habit, and have been exalted to ecstatic song by sudden suffering of some high reality of love. But in our love and our living we also sometimes suffer reality as a deep and deepening wound of disaster, sorrow, and grief. I know I have been stricken, not in any phantasy, but in realness of our human mortality, by such a wound. And often when I have beheld another wounded in our mortal reality, I have been moved to song of compassion.

Once I sang a song for a boy who was mad. He ran away from the hospital in our town in raw cold weather, hoping to find his way home to murder his sister.

> Tall, wind tossed, the wild rust wood
> Stirs on the ridge behind the town;
> With winter sky in squalid mood,
> The woodland floor is blown and brown.

> In a rock-fanged hollow, near its creaking heart,
> By an old green stone, lichen laced,
> Where a rude wind tears dead leaves apart,
> We found the mad boy, awry placed.

> No soul knows which day he died;
> It was not writ on his shrunken nails;
> It must have been while night denied
> Even light and spewed wet gales

That he cowered in covert from terrors near,
There mudded his eyes not to feel the sky,
And died of hunger and cold and fear,
With an unseen shudder and an unheard cry.

Come! Load the winter wind
    With pity's song,
To enwrap the mad boy's soul
    And waft along.

Cheerly voice, above the blast,
    Sweet, strong ditty
To cradle the lorn mad boy
    In endless pity.

Hark! Where thou stridest
    The hollow wind!
Reply! Does our chorale
    Thy pain rescind?

Gone, lad, gone! beyond
    Song's charming;
Cold, lad, cold! beyond
    Tear's warming.

Once I sang a song for a girl who was lovely and young in the
grasp of time; but I met her in the grasp of time, already fearful
of her beauty's change, flying toward passion in fearful flight from
death.

Here comes a girl with laughter in her mouth,
And round the jocund radiance of her brow
She flaunts wild blossoms from a warmer South,
And grows aware that she shall ripen now:
Her startled eyes foresee a mortal trance
In which she'll twine her lovers soon and late;

Her limber body shapes a surgent dance
Of passion sweeping on to procreate:
Her frightened fingers now cannot untie
The rich inweavings of this ripe decay,
Which spins itself from her fertility,
While all her frolic laughter spills away:—
    There was a girl came laughing from the South,—
    Long, long ago a blossom was her mouth.

Once it came upon me how profoundly Shakespeare must have suffered the wound of reality to give forth to us so deep and wondrous song:

You found an hour's torture could be long,
Endured the tedium of a heavy day,
Graced a moment setting down a song,
Unstung a season working out a play;
Abhorred the lips that lured you back to lust,
Grew sick of time that bit into your flesh,
Paid false friend the fatal price of trust,
Crushed your heart through misery's bitter mesh.
Were you happy wishing you could sleep?
Were you happy fabricating kings?
Were you happy in the awesome sweep
Of your own, your wild imaginings?
    We hold your song forever to our heart,
    And have forgot you played the suffering part.

And I met a friend of mine in her garden, whose husband was in prison; she was kneeling on the ground, with her fingers in the earth; and she looked up at me:

    I have thirty flowers
      Bright below a tree;
    Yet not all their powers
      Set him free.

> He was all tomorrow
>   Bright upon my face;
> Now the scorch of sorrow
>   Darks that space.

And once I had a friend who answered me with charm and grace; and once when I spoke to her again she did not answer me, but turned her voice and turned her face and turned herself all away into a silence far from me:

> My friend in space and silence now is drowned,
> Become a strange, uncyphered part of dark,
> Like a tender star that once was found,
> And scarcely found before time quenched her spark;
> My friend is webbed and wound in dread surmise,
> As of a dream of dark that nets the heart
> And curbs its gentle beat with hard surprise;
> Nor can I limn her clear by thought or art;
> I want a music spell, a charm, a prayer—
> I'll try whatever witchery I know—
> To form her bright again in lovely air,
> By word of magic or by word of woe.
>   Shall time and space commit this treachery,
>   To steal my friend, and give back mystery?

And this song of long ago is true in pattern still of other loves that I have lost, and still may lose. For God has given it to the child of my heart to love the child of God in another heart; and often I choose to love, whether I am loved or not. But this song is also true of pain I have wrought in some other heart; for I, too, have failed to answer love, and have turned my voice and turned my face and turned myself away from more than one who offered me trust and love.

Once another was in deep hurt of life at her husband's death, and went on a voyage to rest; and I sent her a song of introduction to Old Ocean, a little song of comfort:

Meet thou this friend of mine with gentle might;
She comes unknowing of thy majestic powers;
Let not thy stormy wilderness affright
A heart deep-needful of thy healing hours.
Show her the splendor of thy massy ways,
Tall cloudy wonders and a singing wind,
And sudden joyance where the dolphin plays,
Then balanced stars that all horizons bind.
Show her thy everlasting age at noon
In the unhurried heaving of thy patient run,
And let her see the evening lift of moon
Follow the wild and smoky set of sun:
    Release strong mystery round thy boundless plain,
    And let her heart be sea-built again.

And once in the West Indies I remembered in song the death
of an emperor:

Black Christophe's bones lie buried near the sea,
Gross weeds and lizards are the green bright wards
That burn on bastions where he used to see
The eyeballs gleaming of his ebon guards;
Torn Haitian clouds weep upon old stone
Reared by his heart for endless majesty;
Down broken halls hot fragrant winds intone
Dark songs of life wrung bare in travesty;
Time gnaws the edges of his dreadful name,
Now near forgot upon his green wild hill,
Leaving the echo of his bare bone shame:
"This Emperor is Death's slave still!"
    Death crushed his joyous ribs in wanton strife,
    And ground to little dust his gorgeous life.

Once I returned from vacation to meet an old farm neighbor,
whom I remembered well in his seasoned vigor and sharp zest
of life; and met him suddenly shrunken and crushed by shock of
suffering:

Now I am old,—
  My wife's gone dead;
We shared forty years
  One great bed.

My clothes hang gaunt,
  My skin hangs slack;
The weight of night
  Weighs my back.

Good God! I'm cold!
  My blood's too slow
To catch a new wife
  With cheeks aglow.

My house is black
  And deadly still:
My old wife's death
  Broke my will.

God damn my fields
  And their bitter stones!
Christ! Give rest
  These old bones!

And I sang an elegy of mute suffering when a widow neighbor of mine died and left her daughter lorn and lone:

My neighbor died the other day. She was old,—
But not so old as her white New England house
On the road beside its small red barns.
I've seen her in her kitchen with her cats—
Grey Persians, except one golden in the band,
All swift and soft at their small leaping—
Her fragile hands and wan anemic face
Were quiet with old weakness nearing death.

I've watched her daughter leading home the cows
When I've been walking in September twilight
(And she and I would always friendly speak);
The cows that hold their evening heads across the gate
Of their hillside pasture, expecting Ruth,
A virgin caught in some day long ago
Where still she walks in peace at simple chores.
And Ruth tonight sits warm alone, quietly
Calling the cats by name around the stove,
Almost hearing the cows stir and breathe greatly
In the small red barn where roosting chickens drowse;
And she remembers with downcast eyes by lamplight
A few last things about her mother who is gone.
And tonight, with first snow fragile on the earth,
The sky is dark, is tender and is strange
With the perpetual wonder of a few first stars,
The way it was the night of the day my mother died.

6 ❧ *Death*

Song and Story

Part One

My suffering at my mother's death was deep and long, a long deep
dwelling in the regions of grief; and one of those who reached his
hand to me and gave me warmth of his life in those breaks of
darkness and steeps of pain was my friend Thomas Wolfe. And
he died.

Sometimes still in the night I dream his face and dream his voice
and dream his great goodness in converse beside me; and again,
after so many years, wake to the knowing of grief that my friend
is dead, waken to the hurt that so deeply hurt him, and the hurt
that hurts me still.

We had much to share in mutual wonder of heart, children both of mountain land, bearing both the mysterious wound of the poet, lovers both of great rhythm and lovely music of word, and trying both to make uttermost gift of heart to others in song. Our friendship was a comfort, one to the other, of two strangely tall men, who beat about the places and times of man and earth, smitten with sorrow and adance with wonder, and trying and trying to tell it, say it, sing it: and he to me and I to him absolutely knew what it was.

"Hello, Tom."

"Hello, Bob."

All the glory of friendship came alive in those small words as Tom and I would say them to one another.

He called himself "God's lonely man." He was haunted by Absence, as if there were never Presence. He sang song of sorrow to God, trying by his prodigious memory to remember God. But when we met, neither one of us was alone, for we met in the deep ranges of intuition and insight, of unknowing and wonder, we met in confirmation of one another, in trust and in song, and the touch of God was with us.

And when he died I wept.

While he lived, I made two songs singing his goodness, and his eyes and his voice were glad while he strode and stood and strode and read them, under the tall ceiling of his bare room in Brooklyn.

After he died, in gratitude and devotion to his memory, I told the story of our friendship in a small book that may one day be published.

And he still companions my spirit in reality of remembrance; the deep grace of his voice, the warm joy of his eye, the trust of his hand, and all his burning torment, too, companion me still, illuminated now by grief.

I

His magic pencil's living poise and slide,
By the late lamplight, across the tablet's face,
Has won from wilderness this giant race

And all the secrets of their hearts descried,
Or did some Angel stoop and long confide
    Into his humble ear the runes of grace
    Whereby this miracle has taken place
Of forming men from words put side by side?
More like, this troubled organ flow of sound,
    This lusty music of a Titan breast,
In which a "Web of Earth" has fitly found
    Its spokesman wrapt in ecstasy, was wrest
In long, lone turmoil from the dark profound
    Where mind and heart and soul secrete their best.

II

Not Prometheus had so proud a tongue,
Nor felt from vulture's beak more bitter woe;
Apollo never was so mad, so young,
Nor made of mortal more immortal throe;
Foam-wreathed Poseidon swayed a calmer sea,
And patient Ceres gleaned more gentle earth,
Venus wove less strenuous mystery,
And Bacchus' ruddy grapes spilled easier mirth;
For these were gods of ancient, sunny hills,
And he is poet forged by wilderness;
Their forms and smiles replied to fated ills,
His joy is torn from dark, flame-fissured stress:
    Heaven again, new trust of God, is won like this,
    When mortal ranges hell, still seeking bliss.

Part Two

My father died when I was a child. The house of my childhood
stood through the years, so long as my mother lived. My mother
died when I was a man.

    The house of my childhood has fallen
      To sorrow and years and pain;
    The roof and the walls are rubble:—
      No anguish shall build it again.

January sunlight flooded my mother's bedroom the day she died. I was the last of those my mother loved to see her alive. She had had a series of strokes which partly paralyzed her and made her at moments insane. In her lucid moments we talked a little; but many times her look and words were insane. I held her hand and talked to her, waiting for her to drowse and rest. She didn't say anything, and I stopped talking. But her eyes were wide open, very brown and luminous eyes, which had beheld and loved so many things, had beheld and even loved me the day I was born, an infant ghastly frail in the grasp of death, and utter pain to behold. We gazed at each other. And for a moment before she closed her eyes forever, they blazed up with a terrible light, wild and insane light, a tremendous shattering of anguish she was communicating to me, a terrible last blaze of dying in the last moment of living; and she died in my living and I lived in her dying; and there was no sound in my living and no sound in her dying. I could not understand the absolute agony that the last light of her eyes said to my heart. She had helped me into my life in a shattering of pain; I helped her into her death in a shattering of compassion. I could not understand her dying or my living; and the compassion of my heart surpassed my understanding. There was no sound in her dying and no sound in my living.

And the ruin of suffering was profound and silent, like ruin and wreck at night on the sea.

> First I gain the beach from wreck and storm
> To lie long stunned and naked on the sand,
> Until a dwindling numbness shapes my form,
> And eyes uplift to see both life and land;
> My mind returns from harsh unquiet ways
> With wounds of death and dreadful mystery,
> Then weary noise of broken-hearted days
> Subsides to stillness deep in memory:
> I gaze in quiet at a petaled flower
> Or at the curious soothing of a shell,
> And feel within my soul renascent power

To rise, to walk, to seek and then to tell:
    Though bitterness and death their noise prolong,
    My quietness enfolds undying song.

And these are the songs I sang, in suffering my mother's death,
in the regions of grief, in the years and the days of so many years:

I

The Lord was your Shepherd,
You shall not want;
But I must find green pastures for myself,
Where not too much blood of war
Shall soak the grass,
Nor fatal gas too much corrupt the wind,—
For the Common Mind now shakes with violence,
And prepares destruction,
That it may build again, blind with hope,
New Agonies;
Or prepares destruction for all mankind
And everywhere,
In despair, never to build again.

Your Redeemer liveth;
His face for you shall be
The quiet face of mercy:
What fair still waters, what fair blue skies
Shall restore your soul,
Fearing no evil in the valley shade,
The green shade,
Until you come to the House of the Lord
Forever.

That green thought in a green shade
Has withered here;
There is no mercy where I am now,
Nor any house in heaven,

And no Lord;
But in the drift of timelessness,
A house of song shall be my dwelling,
And a grave my everlasting home,
And Being shall be my Redeemer
Forever.

For to live at all is strange enough to live forever,
And to sing at all is to sing forever.
You need fear no evil, for He is with you,
And He shall brim your cup with Mercy.

There is no mercy where I am now;
Here the structured world
(Not of earth and seasons, but of Common Mind)
Shakes to bursting, and will burst;
And one strange part never known before,
Some new imperfect mind of old imperfect parts,
Will anneal to think again and fail again
For all mankind:
And Man, too, at some long last,
Shall fail and perish,
Until no star remembers how he sang.
You are waft beside still waters,
And I am left to sing, and sing forever,
Without more soul than the dark wind of death
Can bundle in oblivion.
I have no Shepherd,—
Where I am now three Dreams,
Dream of Terror, Dream of Guilt, and Dream of Ruin
Can shepherd a man into oblivion.
When my brain is broken,
And my flesh untied from my bones,
I shall not want and shall not dream;
But now I am,—

And to be is to be in want forever,
And to dream,
With no surcease but song,
And no surcease but death.

I am lost to God. I am delivered
Unto the dust of death.
In the maze of Agony I have lost my God,
And am delivered unto dust of death.

II

When the wind rises up the boughs of the pine
    And shakes it from bottom to top;
When the wind redoubles its fretful whine
    After a fitful stop,—

I remember the loud return
    Of a near forgotten grief;
And I forget the silentness
    Of infinite relief.

III

I met Necessity so long ago
That he has always been my mortal brother;
And I have found no solitude in woe,
For there I saw his face and saw no other.

He lets me wear the eager mask, in vain,
Of love-sweet nights and proud ambitious days;
He prods my feet to dance designs of pain
On tables old of antique human ways.

Necessity is blind, but I can see
I shall at last elude his fierce embrace,
And shape a zero out of misery,
When I am dust on death's great quiet face.

I am here to learn the worth
    Of your returning never.

I shall watch the fireflies
    Weave darkness down the valley:
I shall hear the waterfalls
    Make echo echo rally.

I cannot draw you free of death
    By force of long despairing,—
Soon I'll take a startled breath,
To some new joy repairing.

VII

Rest, now, my mother, let the ancient earth
Be the home of your heart forever.

I can remember how you loved the earth:
    Wake, now, my heart, from moody sorrow wake!
      My heart, be happy where the river bends;
In hollow dell soft loosen laughter's girth,
    Rival the thrush across the evening lake,
      Give to jubilance all that sorrow lends;
    Go singing past the windy, buxom fields,
      Rejoice where the mazy, murmuring forest ends,
    Pour into singing all disaster yields;
My heart, be mirthful where the sea spray splashes,
    From stony crags wring echoes of delight,
      Sing at heaven where the foul storms mass,
Nor yet be still when the thunder crashes:
    My mother, walk upon the earth in light,
      In easy motion like the wind-bent grass:
My mother, sleep; your shape has fallen to ashes.

The drowsy fullness of the day shall sink
    Within the orchard, where the fireflies

Shall weave the fallen night to darkness;
And lovely Night shall tread across the brink
Of far, dun hills, unscarf her darkling eyes,
And net the slumb'rous land in her heart's dark fastness;
She'll call the quiring stars to sing and burn
Throughout heaven's bays and arching vastness,
And bid the full fair moon once more return;
But you who sleep forever have no need
Of Night; your eyes are dust, and cannot see
The mountain-mottled circle of the moon
Roving slow among the starry seed
To measure Time and Darkness leisurely:
You sleep forever; oh! you sleep too soon!
Wake! Wake! Gone eternally!

No morning meadow, where the day scents rise
And sway my living sense to sudden song
Can rouse again your gentle fallen head;
No wild bird singing out in spring surprise
So that the day would fain itself prolong
Can reach your silence down among the dead;
And no strange light of evenfall at sea,
Filtering its way to my living heart, shall spread
Your drowsy lids weighed down eternally;
No potion wrung from cool and clustered grapes,
No sap of fruit, no earth-deep sparkling spring
Could stir your tongue to momentary breath;
And my lamenting hand, though sorrow drapes
Each finger with the bloom of long despairing,
Cannot sweep your fallen brow of death,
Nor lure you back to sense and former being.

Rest, now, my mother; now the ancient earth
Is the home of your heart forever.

IX

I remember how you loved the earth!
Once where the mazy murmuring forest ends,
Where the crystal stream redoubles its bubbling birth,
Where the mountain lily turns in the breeze and bends,
The mellow light placed beauty on your face;
Once by buxom fields, where shadows pass,
Where the meadow lark weaves her song in golden grace,
Your step was easy through the wind-bent grass;
Once you loved the sunny space of noon,
Once eventide enlarged your happy eyes,
Among the mountains once you traced the moon,
Once smiled to watch the frolic fireflies:
    Your lovely pleasure of the earth shall store
    My soul of solitude forevermore.

X

I met thee, caught of fear, bereft of song,
Eyes hurt, on path of terror, dark and bright;
Implored thou me: "What shall I do?—so long
Afeared in cross and cross of tragic light!"

      Thyself was song, where the dark wind blows,
        And all thy grace shone clear and near;
      I spoke a word love instant knows:
        "I am thy son. I hold thee dear."

XI

How good it is to be a limber reed,
Rooted, and wild in sweet responsive flash
To the divine blowing of our daily meed,—
Rooted in God, and unafraid of brash
And blowing wondrous winds or sudden light
That burst like fire and music out of earth,

And sweep my spirit with new-create delight,
Refreshing every moment with an holy birth!
O, thus to be a man of earth and God,
With root in Being, and being formed for song,
A singing reed upsprung from hallowed Sod,—
This joy that God began, love long prolong!
    Sweet glory is it, that a man so springs,
    Upward grows in radiant light, and sings!

7   Gratitude, Suffering, and Love

An Affirmation

I concede my heart to joy and to tragedy, and I sing.

I rejoice where I love, at any life fulfilled.

I suffer where I love, at any break of life between myself and anyone I love, be it little pain of unkindness or terrible pain of death. I suffer most where I love the most; and thou most tender to me, mother, father, wife, child, friend, can by any break of life between us make me suffer deeply; and if I break life between us I suffer deeply, too. And the deepest wound of all my life is in my love of God, that I have broken life before His face. Yea, though Thou slay me, I still shall sing in gratitude and still shall love Thee, for Thou hast made me; Thou art my God in all my knowing, and beyond all my knowing Thou art my God. And when in the maze of agony at last I meet with Thee, the illumination of gratitude breaks the heart of agony and restores the heart of peace.

The life of a man is a smile of God. The life of a man is Thy beatitude.

I am Thy child, and I shall love Thee.

I concede my life to joy and to tragedy, and I sing.

And so I sing of gratitude, in a world so full of pain.

Book Seven

The Beatitude
of a Lived Life

1 🙢🙠 Do You Know the Wind

A Vision

Do you know the wind blowing at night among all the stars? Who can rise in the morning and step out on the earth in the mist before dawn, and say it is himself that established the earth and brings on the day? Do you rise in the morning and step out on the earth in the mist before dawn, and rejoice in the Other, Who brings on the day? Who shall ever disclose his full gratitude for the abundance of God in the night and the day? Our earth is one of the stars among all the stars of heaven, and, in truth, there is no other place but heaven and no other time but eternity. How shall the heart of a man be great enough to rejoice in his gratitude for the abundance of God? How shall the voice of a man be tender enough to sing of his consonance with God?

2 🙢🙠 Songs to God

A Meditation

To sing differently to God is not less to sing to God.

The life of each man and each woman and each child is a song to God.

Who among men has most beautifully sung to God I shall never know. But many songs of many men to God have touched and uplifted my heart. Certainly the song of Aeschylus rings out deep and strong, and clear and lovely is the song that Botticelli sang; and a great chorus of now nameless men and women and children sang that heart-lifting song in stone and glass that is Chartres Cathedral.

169

Each of us needs to find his own song to God and entrust his life to singing it as well as he is able.

I love Dante's *Vita Nuova,* his song of youthful tears and gratitude and yearning for immortal grace, and all his exalted rainbow love for Beatrice, unattainable and unattained. And the great song of all his life, Inferno, Purgatorio, Paradiso, was singing still in raptured gaze toward Beatrice, his exalted dream of woman —*"la bella donna della mia mente"*—lovely, unattainable, and never so mortal as to clasp his hand in mortal ways, but forever dreamed. And his great song rose in exalted gratitude to where all the stars sang.

But I am not so moved by youth's exalted imagining, and cannot sing of youth's immortal desire to worship removed and untouchable beauty. For God touched my heart the morning of my birth, when I lay dying, and He has been my Eternal Thou since my beginning, binding me in compassion to our world and our human bondage.

I love the singing gratitude of David in his Psalms. I love his passion, sounding the trouble and joy of his grateful heart to God, his great song of trust and covenant in recurring crisis of passion and pride and power, compassed about by enemies and hot bulls of Bashan, the waters come in unto his soul, his throat dried out with crying, delivered into the dust of death, still trusting God our God, blessing God our God, and lying down in the mercy of green pastures, beside the comfort of still waters, and fearing no evil, for God our God was with him.

But I have never had any dominion or power, and no enemies have encompassed me, and I could not sing the great song of one of God's anointed kings, even though the waters have come in unto my soul until I was overwhelmed in my crying, and stood in the dust of death, and waited for God our God in dark night of soul, and was healed and lifted up to open my heart and sing.

One of the most beautiful songs to God that I ever heard was sung to God in the night by a Navajo Indian woman, standing alone in the red and roaming light of a circle of great bonfires.

It was on broad land among mesas at Gallup, New Mexico, with the far shapes of mesas massy under the brilliant stars. She was singing a song of her people, but she was singing the song of her life to God. In the name of her people, and blessing each of a thousand strangers who heard her, she lifted up her life, totally given to God, in beauty and joy, lovely and upright upon the earth and among all the stars.

No man ever lived who could sing that exalted song of woman, mother of people, blessing God for gift and nurture of life.

I could never sing as the Indian woman sang, and lifted up my heart to life.

I cannot sing as Dante sang, of exalted Beauty and implacable Justice; nor sing as David sang, in anointed covenant with God; nor sing St. Francis' sweet joy in seeking every wound of his Master's Cross; nor sing Bach's harmonious immortal converse with God, nor Beethoven's tragic and tender compassion with God.

Each man may sing his own song of heart to God, and each true song of heart is holy.

I am an old man of our common human bondage, touched in my mortal heart by God to sing the beatitude of my lived life. I sing the beatitude of a humble life, never emblazoned with glories or powers, obscure, uncertain, often rejected and disapproved, often ashamed, deep in failure, a common life of love and suffering and gratitude. And each of my loves has taught me deeper joy and deeper pain of song.

I had to visit the deepest wound of all my life, and stand there, and be there, and pray there, before I could concede my heart to joy and to tragedy and sing this my song in praise of gratitude, with all God's creation of all my years burned into me and brought to the beatitude of a lived life.

The deepest wound of all my life is in my love of God.

How strange a thing to sing!

Should it not be some horrid stroke, delivered against me by evil? Should it not be some towering horrid crime, committed by me in rage of evil?

How should a man be so wounded in his love of God that no other wound surpasses it?

I cannot explain the mystery of my own love for God, but only live it, only sing it.

The deepest wound of all my life is in my love of God, that I have broken life before His face, broken trust in life before His face. On a thousand days, in a thousand little ways, I have broken trust in life before the face of God.

And again and again He has healed me, and He has taught me deeper joy and deeper pain of song.

And it is for me to sing beatitude of a lived life.

3 🐾 *The Beatitude of a Lived Life*

An Essay

The beatitude of a lived life is to become a person of God and a companion of God. We know from experience what it is to become a person and a companion in our family, in our town, in our society. First we must become real and present as a person, as whole as we are able, and hiding behind no masks of hypocrisy, no pretended pieties, and with no concealed or predatory purposes; then we must walk together with others in communion of word and work and venture. This is our humble hallowing of the days of our life with and for one another. And to become a person of God and a companion of God is, in truth, the beatitude of this hallowing placed upon our lives. The generations of men that have known this are many, and it was said of old by Micah: "He hath shewed thee, O man, what is good; and what doth the Lord require of thee, but to do justly, to love mercy, and to walk humbly with thy God?"

There is a City of God, shining near at hand beside us, glowing and warm within us, where God invites our companionship; and we could pick up the bundle of all our life and enter into it with rejoicing song of gratitude to dwell there a person of God in His companionship; we need but direct the steps of our heart toward Him. But what thousands of days we dwell alone in dark closets of busyness, hurry, convenience, in dreary shantytowns of lust, pride, sloth, in weary wastelands of doubt and despair, all on the verges of this shining home, dwell apart from God, breaking life in the face of God, scarcely knowing how deep a wound we have taken into our own heart!

I think each man could tell, if he would, many and many a moment when the deepest wound of all his life suddenly again became real and terrible in his own knowing. Sometimes it is like a dark storm of sudden anguish. Sometimes it is a creeping paralysis of despair. Sometimes it is terror at the shoulder. Has your conscience sometime told you: "You are the one who has broken life?" How common it is that prudence advises us, convenience urges us on, and comfort of profit closes the deal, and wraps us up in darkness with it. It was not the storm of circumstance that swept into your heart the waters and the weariness of disappointment, the dust and dryness of death. Are you the one to be the master and arbiter of reality? Your conscience knows and tells that it was you, drunken in your own pride or fear or anger or disgust, who threw a stone at a flower, threw a stone at a dog, threw a stone at a friend, threw a stone at God. To have your power fringed by being less than God is to be the mortal you are, and no wound. To have your gratitude refused is indeed painful frustration; but to be yourself not grateful and throw a stone at God is the deeper wound.

Any stone I throw at God strikes into my own heart and bruises a jagged wound. All the stones I have thrown at God have made this the most terrible wound of all my life. And only God can heal it. For I love God, and I have broken life in His face. Only God, accepting the turning of my heart in gratitude and my heart blessing God, can heal my deepest wound.

And I think each man could sing, if he would, many and many a moment when, standing in prayer in the deepest wound of all his life, he felt God once more touch and heal his heart in companionship and he became again a person of God in the beatitude of a lived life, and rejoicing in gratitude he entered the City of God. If we could dwell there forever in companionship with God, we would be immortal; we are mortal, imperfect and frail, and can only return again and again, until finally it is the beatitude of our lived life that we have tried to live and perhaps really have lived withal more a person and companion of God in the City of God, and less a wounded self-blinded self on the verge of it, more devoutly God's and less passionately our own.

By return and return to God, a lived life not entirely holy, sometimes tragically unholy, still in our human measure made immeasurable by God's mercy, becomes the beatitude of a lived life.

I shall tell of one such moment of turn and return, rising to song, from my own life. It is one of those moments when, in the deepening of years, all love returns in a deepening of love and all suffering returns in a deepening of suffering, and my thousand ventures of love and suffering utterly render known to me the deepest wound of all my life, that only God can heal.

4 A Moment of Blessing

Prayer and Mystery

However many other ways I might tell and sing it, I tell and sing it now in a story and song of fifty years, and even eight more to the morning of my birth. That is sweep enough of mortal time and human bondage to image wound and gratitude and becoming once more a person and companion of God in the beatitude of a lived life.

My father died over fifty years ago, in the spring, when I was a child of eight, and light was cool in the evening time in the month of March, where we lived in Santa Fe, New Mexico. I went into the orchard among the bare small apple trees and lifted up my arms, asking heaven for my father; and there was no sound, and my arms fell, and a killdeer wheeled and cried. And suffering, which I already knew from birth, the mute suffering of a premature, flaw-hearted, and dying child, deepened within my heart, to be with me, deepening still, for all my life.

And a profound motion and turning toward another in love happened to me then, like a deep and silent direction in my life, that I did not fully know and understand and sing until dawn of Easter morning fifty years later, in April of the year 1960.

This was a spring when two I loved who had meant much to me during many years of my life lay dying, a woman I loved and a man I loved; and when I visited now one, now the other, they were passing further and further beyond the verges of communication into the throes and silences of death. They had been a comfort to me for thirty-five years and for forty years. Neither the woman nor the man had ever spoken to me or behaved toward me except in trust and kindness; and I had tried to be as true as that to them. Now they moved in suffering into death, and their suffering moved me.

The last time I saw the man in consciousness, though I visited him several more times in his unconsciousness, I stood by his bed, clasped his hand, and bending over kissed him on his forehead; and he opened his eyes for a steady moment and gently said:

"Thanks, boy."

The last time I saw the woman in consciousness, though I visited her several times more in her unconsciousness, I sat beside her bed and held her hand, and suddenly she clasped my hand very tight, and I held tight, and she said:

"Don't let me fall from this terrible place!"

And then and later, as I clasped the hands of these two who were dying, as I kissed their silent foreheads, I was deeply moved with new understanding of how sacred is our communication and our presence to one another, in any help at any time and for as long as we can give it, and how grievous a wrong it is ever to break life between myself and another by any will or choosing of my own. Entering into the presence of these two who were now dying also turned my heart more, and more tenderly, in gratitude toward each one I love.

But this sharing in the death of two I loved brought back in tides of suffering all the deaths in all the breaks in life in all my loves, and most profoundly returned me to the terrible moment when my mother died in my living, and I lived in her dying, and there was no sound between us. And all the earth and skies of my heart were lit by the terrible fire of the last blaze of agony in her dying eyes as we gazed at one another. It was soundless music of the most terrible song to God I have ever heard, and it had broken my heart open to the grief of God; for the song of the last light of my mother's eyes was this:

"Oh, child, my child! Art thou my death! Oh, God, my God! Deliver my child from this agony of my death!"

And with a broken heart she laid down her life in my living, without a sound. And I shall never hear a more terrible song to God. That was twenty-five years ago; but there is no time except eternity; and all my loves and all my sufferings once more now were set in eternity, in a profound abyss of present pain, under that terrible light and tremendous music of agony illuminating the earth and skies of my heart.

All my failures returned, the thousand and thousand times when I had broken life between myself and some other one I loved, when I loved God and yet broke life in His face. So many days have I made unholy by muttering misery in the sun; so many words have I poisoned with pride, coldness, and anger, setting death in some other heart; so many works have I corrupted with greed or resentment or sloth, abusing the abundance of God like a vandal or a wastrel; so many times have I hurt someone who loved me by being less than a person and companion of God in their presence; so many times have I turned into dark and solitary confinement of self alone, denying God.

In the fullness of my years, in the return of my failures, the return of the tides of love and of suffering were deep and over-whelming, and the depth of the deepest wound of all my life was profound and shattering. My oldest pain and my newest pain were one; my first day and this day were one. And death resounded in my days and my doings. While spring came on and the daffodils bloomed in our orchard, death resounded in my days and my doings.

And my conscience told me: "Thou art the one who has broken life in the face of God." Can you demand that another shall never die? Are you to command that anyone, or any other one, or yourself, is to be forever young, and not have lived? Can you demand that your will be done? Are you too good to open your heart to the asking need of another? You rage in your heart, and squat and rot alone in yourself, in your arrogance to be the perfect one, denying God because you fear the humble receiving of His mercy. He made you. He knows you are mortal, frail, and needy and would heal you in hallowed meeting. "Thou art the one who has beggared thyself before God, and made thyself unfit to be His companion. Stop telling thy queasy misery and fat-eyed pride to thyself. *Turn! Turn!* Go lift and tell thy joy of heart to God!"

And the mercy of truth enlightened the just rebuke of my conscience.

On a clear day—it happened to be Good Friday—I woke from my nap, saying aloud to myself where I lay:

"I will go into the woods by Roxbury Falls, and pray."

I happened to be alone in the house, even as I was alone in my wound. My wife was in New York at a performance of *Parsifal,* and our children and grandchildren were in cities far off. The rooms of our home were silent in sunlight.

I drove in my car the fifteen miles or so to Roxbury Falls, left the car, crossed the bridge, and entered the woods.

It is a lovely place in my life and in the lives of my wife and children. We have been there many a time to picnic and swim, and many a time no one else was there. It is a place hallowed for me by the joy of my wife and the laughter of my children, and I have taken my grandchildren there to frolic and swim, to make and sail little boats and sing.

The small river comes down a deep cleft of rocky walls and lunges and plunges over great stone; and large hemlocks and lesser trees stand on the high ledges on either side of the little gorge. Light and shadow flash and play on forest, stone, and water.

I sat on the floor of hemlock needles and leaned my back against ledge stone, and there in the wound of all my life I prayed without praying, I simply was there and listened and waited. I had no conscious intent of listening and waiting; perhaps as an infant child, too weak either to cry or to smile, or to lift my hand, and sometimes in coma, my first lesson in life was to listen and wait for touch of life to touch me. I breathed the lovely air, fragrant of wood and water, earth and stone; I watched the little moving of the boughs of trees showing patches of sapphire sky, and watched and listened to the lively tumble of the waters over the stones. I remembered such a day years ago when I had come there alone and stripped off my clothes and sported flashing and gleaming in and under the water and let its surges break upon my shoulders and played with the froth and the bubbles.

A tall boy and a girl nearly as tall came into the woods, both dressed in gay shirts and dark-blue shorts, holding hands. Their bright faces and bare arms and bare legs shone, and their springing bodies were all eager, lithe, and young. They glanced at me, startled, quickly; then quickly and eagerly glanced away in communion of lovers forgetting anyone else is there. Hand in hand, hip brushing hip in their happy motion, they strolled on into the woods, turning out of sight, into their own springtime forest dream and seeking of love; and the wings of Eros were in the woodland in the fragrant air.

Nothing happened to me, except a deepened stillness of being. And I did nothing. There was nothing I could do, being where I was, as I was, one who loved God and had broken life in His face. I was too deep in all my loss of love, too weak in all my failure and pain, to pronounce myself. It was very like the morning of my birth in April fifty-eight years before, when I came broken and flawed into the light of day with no birthright to live out the morning of my birth, too weak in the grasp of death to pronounce myself, and I could not cry and could not smile and barely had faint strength to breathe; and only the touch of God stayed me in life a while to become a man and sing.

The grace of quietness filled all the air among the trees, and sunlight sparkled on the dancing water. The soundless and re-sounding music of God was forever and everywhere. And I lost the loneliness of being myself, a separate self alone, and making no sound at all, I also joined in song. And the palms of my hands lay and softly stirred against the smooth needles and aromatic sponge of the woodland floor, in caress between earth and man.

And after simply being there where I was, as I was, for an hour in the woods at Roxbury Falls, I rose and started to move away. But then I turned to look at the falls again. I stood between two small trees under greater trees and looked at the falls again, and held a hand on each of the trees.

I was immeasurably not alone.

"Upon Thee was I cast at my birth, and since my mother bore me, Thou hast been my God."

To the tree on which the palm of my left hand pressed, I said, "Bless thee, tree."

To the tree on which the palm of my right hand pressed, I said,

"Thou tree, be blessed."

And the trees and I stood under greater trees on the ledge above the waterfall. And we were immeasurably not alone.

A quietness too quiet for me to know it was there met me and lifted me up into new creation.

How shall the heart of a man be great enough to rejoice in his gratitude for the abundance of God? How shall the voice of a man be tender enough to sing of his healing consonance with God?

At dawn of Easter morning I sang a song of recollection of my childhood, of meeting my mother at the time of my father's death, so long ago:

I met thee, caught of fear, bereft of song,
Eyes hurt, on path of terror, dark and bright;
Implored thou me: "What shall I do?—so long
Afeared in cross and cross of tragic light!"

Thyself was song, where the dark wind blows,
    And all thy grace shone clear and near;
I spoke a word love instant knows:
    "I am thy son. I hold thee dear."

How strange it is that a song, rising to music in our own heart, until we sing it out in giving of our life—that song then shines back and illuminates the depths and years of our own life!

Singing this song in remembrance of my mother shone upon all my years, and I knew I had answered with fifty years of my life and all the compassion of my heart to the outcry of my mother's fear and grief in her shock of suffering when my father died. And I knew that this was good, a deep direction and stream of never having entirely broken life in the face of God, of never having entirely failed to turn and try to give comfort, not only to my mother but to anyone and many a one met in the hurt of life. A touch of God in my childhood had set a seal upon my life, the seal and commitment to try to learn so to love as to break the heart of agony and restore the heart of peace, to try to learn so to love God as to spread peace. In gratitude to His mercy to me, that I had lived at all, I was committed to lift up my heart and spread peace. And this was what I was forced to sing, and to sing in praise of gratitude. That had happened to me as a child, for all my life, that made me devoutly God's and less passionately my own. Often the joy had been very sweet, sweet in communion with others, in all mutual hallowing and tenderness and loyalties of a lived life; and often the pain had been very great in the griefs of mortality and in the failings and breakings of life. I had loved where I was loved; I had failed where I was loved; I had loved where I was not loved. And it was good that I had lived. And all my loves of all my life were set in my love of God.

The quietness of meeting God had once more entered into me and once more healed the deepest wound of all my life; and once again, become a person and companion of God by a touch beyond my knowing. I had been brought by Him in unto the beatitude of a lived life.

And it was a very good thing to be grateful to have been only myself, only this man I am—and not any other and not a wan dream self-imposed or imposed by any other—but this one man into whom God had burned the infinite mercy and abundance of His creation, including my failures and my sufferings, including my aspirations and my joys and my loves. It was a very good thing to have become this man, given into life by God.

The beatitude of my lived life is humble, plain, and common.

I have lived in the good human bondage of the generations of man.

I have been the child of my parents, husband to my wife, father to my children, and grandfather to those arising, sons of God and mothers of people, and a friend to many friends, and sometimes a comforter of strangers.

And I have had to learn, in grief and compassion, to be a not wanted person, and still to love each one who teaches me this heavy lesson.

And I have listened to the music of God, and sung a man's song as well as I could.

And my gratitude is very great.

I once more sing my song of heart.

And in my knowing and in my unknowing I bless God.

Book Eight

Song of Heart

1 ❧ Appointment with God

A man's life is an appointment with God.

It has been the essence of my appointment with God to live a life ordinary and obscure, but of intense spiritual toil for vision and song. I have been given to live bewildered and unknowing in the painful tensions of failure and the joyous sweeps of mystery and, so living, been given to lift up my heart and sing. I have tried to live my life in sweet courtesy toward earth and creature and people and God, and to sing in gratitude that it has been good. It is the beatitude of my lived life that I have tried to concede my life to joy and to tragedy, and to sing, and that way tried to fulfill my appointment with God.

2 ❧ Immeasurably Not Alone

I could never sing alone.

Many others and God have helped me.

And it is good to have stood long enough in life to have found courage and gratitude in my heart to sing for others and to God the deepest song of my heart. The song is not made by me, but given through me. I have tried to be faithful to the great Music through which it is given.

Gratitude is my deepest song of heart.

And I sing my song of heart immeasurably not alone.

3 ❧ Music of God

*That has happened to me which makes me more devoutly God's
and less passionately my own;*
  I am broken open by the music of God;
  And I am become an old man in the beatitude of a lived life;
  And my song of heart is gratitude to God for all my life;
  And I offer my song of heart among men, in the watch of God;
  *And God shall hear the song of heart I sing to men, for a man
—and for a woman—and for a child.*

4 ❧ To Each One I Love

    Thou art my friend, and I shall hold thee dear
    In gentle ways that beat dread darkness down;
    I met thee in the peace of "God is here!"
    And shall not hide from God what is His own.

    I know our day of darkened soul distraught,
    Cloyed full of easements down into despair,
    In evil swirl of violence overtaught,
    And sleazy horror haunting everywhere.

    It is my simple thing to lift my face
    So thou shalt know that thou hast met a friend
    Within God's watch of living peace and grace:—
    When two have met with God is horror's end.

      Look for God's legend always in my eye:
      Abide in my heart at peace until I die.

5 ❧ Word of Man

Here is the simple word of my given life,
Wrought in the joy and loss of love and pain,
Wrung from fall and failure, full steeped in strife,
As terrible as fire, and as soft as rain;

A word hard hammered on the evil stone
Of fear and passion at the heart of hell,
But tender with rejoicing of my love and bone,—
Made holy by the grief in which we dwell;

It is the word I offer to thy soul,
As real as rest, as sure as healing song:—
Let thy receiving make my giving whole,
In mutual trust by which we both grow strong:

Ask thou my word for all there is of me,
As thou I ask thy simple word of thee.

6 ❧ Sudden Song

How good it is to be a limber reed,
Rooted, and wild in sweet responsive flash
To the divine blowing of our daily meed,—
Rooted in God, and unafraid of brash

And blowing wondrous winds or sudden light
That burst like fire and music out of earth,
And sweep my spirit with new-create delight,
Refreshing every moment with an holy birth!

O, thus to be a man of earth and God,
With root in Being, and being formed for song,
A singing reed upsprung from hallowed Sod,—
This joy that God began, love long prolong!

Sweet glory is it, that a man so springs,
Upward grows in radiant light, and sings!

7 🌿 God Is Our God

"Let us take sweet counsel together, and walk toward the house of God."

For God is our God in all our knowing; and beyond all our knowing, God is our God.

And gratitude shall be the miracle of our communion.

Gratitude shall be the miracle that hallows our communion and our love in the touch of God.

Gratitude shall be our home in the presence of God.

And we shall bless God.

INDEX OF SONGS

(In Order of Appearance)

190   *In Praise of Gratitude*

Set in Garamond
Format by Leonore Troost-Falck
Manufactured by The Haddon Craftsmen, Inc.
Published by HARPER & BROTHERS, *New York*